Samuel French Acting Edition

The Safety Net

by Christopher Kyle

‖SAMUEL FRENCH‖

Copyright © 2007 by Wiggle, Inc. f/s/o Christopher Kyle
All Rights Reserved

THE SAFETY NET is fully protected under the copyright laws of the United States of America, the British Commonwealth, including Canada, and all member countries of the Berne Convention for the Protection of Literary and Artistic Works, the Universal Copyright Convention, and/or the World Trade Organization conforming to the Agreement on Trade Related Aspects of Intellectual Property Rights. All rights, including professional and amateur stage productions, recitation, lecturing, public reading, motion picture, radio broadcasting, television, online/digital production, and the rights of translation into foreign languages are strictly reserved.

ISBN 978-0-573-63385-0

www.concordtheatricals.com
www.concordtheatricals.co.uk

FOR PRODUCTION INQUIRIES

UNITED STATES AND CANADA
info@concordtheatricals.com
1-866-979-0447

UNITED KINGDOM AND EUROPE
licensing@concordtheatricals.co.uk
020-7054-7200

Each title is subject to availability from Concord Theatricals Corp., depending upon country of performance. Please be aware that *THE SAFETY NET* may not be licensed by Concord Theatricals Corp. in your territory. Professional and amateur producers should contact the nearest Concord Theatricals Corp. office or licensing partner to verify availability.

CAUTION: Professional and amateur producers are hereby warned that *THE SAFETY NET* is subject to a licensing fee. The purchase, renting, lending or use of this book does not constitute a license to perform this title(s), which license must be obtained from Concord Theatricals Corp. prior to any performance. Performance of this title(s) without a license is a violation of federal law and may subject the producer and/or presenter of such performances to civil penalties. Both amateurs and professionals considering a production are strongly advised to apply to the appropriate agent before starting rehearsals, advertising, or booking a theatre. A licensing fee must be paid whether the title(s) is presented for charity or gain and whether or not admission is charged. Professional/Stock licensing fees are quoted upon application to Concord Theatricals Corp.

This work is published by Samuel French, an imprint of Concord Theatricals Corp.

No one shall make any changes in this title(s) for the purpose of production. No part of this book may be reproduced, stored in a retrieval system, scanned, uploaded, or transmitted in any form, by any means, now known or yet to be invented, including mechanical, electronic, digital, photocopying, recording, videotaping, or otherwise, without the prior written permission of the publisher. No one shall share this title(s), or any part of this title(s), through any social media or file hosting websites.

For all inquiries regarding motion picture, television, online/digital and other media rights, please contact Concord Theatricals Corp.

MUSIC AND THIRD PARTY MATERIALS USE NOTE

Licensees are solely responsible for obtaining formal written permission from copyright owners to use copyrighted music and/or other copyrighted third-party materials (e.g., artworks, logos) in the performance of this play and are strongly cautioned to do so. If no such permission is obtained by the licensee, then the licensee must use only original music and materials that the licensee owns and controls. Licensees are solely responsible and liable for clearances of all third-party copyrighted materials, including without limitation music, and shall indemnify the copyright owners of the play(s) and their licensing agent, Concord Theatricals Corp., against any costs, expenses, losses and liabilities arising from the use of such copyrighted third-party materials by licensees. For music, please contact the appropriate music licensing authority in your territory for the rights to any incidental music.

IMPORTANT BILLING AND CREDIT REQUIREMENTS

If you have obtained performance rights to this title, please refer to your licensing agreement for important billing and credit requirements.

THE SAFETY NET was produced by Broken Watch Theatre Company (Drew DeCorleto, Artistic Director; Leo Lauer, Executive Director) at the Michael Weller Theatre in New York City on September 19, 2005. It was directed by Martha Banta; the set design was by J. Wiese; the lighting design was by Miriam Nilofa Crowe; the sound design was by Jill BC DuBoff; the costume design was by Cora Levin and the production stage manager was Joan Cappello. The cast was as follows:

DAVID .... Jason Pugatch
SONYA .... Eva Kaminsky
RICK .... Mark Setlock
LASHONDA .... Tinashe Kajese
DEB .... Maren Perry
TRUDY .... Peggy Scott

CAST OF CHARACTERS

DAVID, white, mid 30s
SONYA, white, mid 30s
RICK, white, mid 30s
LASHONDA, black, early 20s
TRUDY, white, 60ish
DEB, white, late 40s

SETTING

Various locations in New York City, Maine and Indiana. It is important that David be able to move fluidly from one scene to another without blackouts, so the locations may be suggested minimally.

SPECIAL THANKS
THE SAFETY NET was written with generous support from the John Simon Guggenheim Memorial Foundation and was developed at New York Theatre Workshop, Playwrights Horizons, Seattle Repertory Theatre, Charlotte Repertory Theatre, Hudson Stage Company and Indiana State University.

For Josh.

ACT I

(One. Lights rise on DAVID and SONYA's apartment. A coat rack. DAVID, in a dark suit, stands at a mirror contemplating neckties. SONYA ENTERS in a robe.)

SONYA. It's today, isn't it?
DAVID. Yes.
SONYA. I forgot.

(She EXITS. DAVID yanks off the necktie he just put on and throws it on the floor.)

DAVID. Damn it.

(He tries on another. SONYA returns with coffee.)

SONYA. We're out of soymilk and I don't really trust this lactose-free stuff. I'm sorry, David. About forgetting.
DAVID. Maybe I should save this tie for my own funeral. *(Unknots it.)* Would you pick? They all look the same to me.

(SONYA looks them over, then picks up the tie David threw on the floor. He puts it on.)

SONYA. If I were a lawyer I couldn't bear getting dressed.

THE SAFETY NET

DAVID. After I make partner I can spice it up a little. On Fridays you often see the partners in golfing clothes— plaid pants, white shoes, one of those crushable caps... Not so stuffy.

SONYA. I'm looking forward to that.

DAVID. Yesterday Melanie as much as said I'm in— as much as said I'll make partner next year. Of course, she's not above intrigue. Telling me I might get overconfident, slack off a bit. She has a Byzantine soul.

SONYA. You wouldn't slack off.

DAVID. Not with a crushable cap on my horizon. This goes together?

SONYA. It might be flashy, under the circumstances.

DAVID. What about the blue one?

SONYA. I was teasing.

DAVID. Right.

SONYA. *(Adjusting his collar.)* You're not really going to wear one of those hats.

DAVID. Only if I lose my hair. *(Kisses her.)*

SONYA. Are you worried about making partner, sweetheart?

DAVID. It's in the bag.

SONYA. So what was that look?

DAVID. What look?

SONYA. Is something wrong?

DAVID. I just remembered a client who needs my love. I can call him from the plane.

(He EXITS, then returns with toiletries and packs through the following.)

SONYA. You want to hear something insane? On the subway yesterday this black kid was going in and out the door between the cars, slamming it, you know, letting in the screech of the wheels,

THE SAFETY NET

and I found myself hoping he'd fall between the cars and be killed. He was quite smug. But while I was thinking about the wheels thumping over him and wondering if it was because I was really that angry or was it maybe I just need more, I don't know, for lack of a better word, meaning in my life, it finally occurred to me that if he were crushed under the wheels the train would be delayed for hours. Hours. And I was already late. So you see— no matter what happened he had me beat. If he were crushed, obviously, they'd do an investigation, interview everyone on the train, and I was afraid in a moment of weakness I might admit to hoping he'd fall and then I'd become a social outcast. It scared me because my wanting him to die had nothing to do with race.

DAVID. You're not liable for your thoughts, Sonya. Especially on the subway.

SONYA. Do you ever feel like we're just sitting next to each other on a plane, passing time, amusing each other, but when we land we'll go in opposite directions and never meet again?

DAVID. Are you back in therapy?

SONYA. It's not like that, David; it's real. Sometimes I'm afraid.

DAVID. Of what?

SONYA. Of what you're really thinking when you get those looks.

DAVID. Why don't we drive up to Maine this weekend, up to that bed and breakfast with the organic cows— remember?

SONYA. Of course I remember. That's the place you took me to forget about my hystericalectomy. And it wasn't the cows we liked, it was the view. The ocean was very soothing.

DAVID. I was looking at the cows.

SONYA. Do I worry you, David? Am I showing signs?

DAVID. I didn't say that. We can go if it will make you feel better.

SONYA. It's not just me, David. It's us.

THE SAFETY NET

DAVID. That's what I meant. *(Looks outside.)* My car is here.
SONYA. He's early.
DAVID. I'll barely make the service as it is.
SONYA. You're not cutting it short on my account, are you? Maybe you want to spend more time with your parents.
DAVID. If they had a flight I'd come back this evening.
SONYA. It's going to look odd, isn't it? My absence.
DAVID. They know you hate to fly.
SONYA. I keep picturing everyone gathered around the receptacle, the urn, but there's this gap among the mourners, a sucking hole called Sonya.
DAVID. The whole event is rushed anyway. My father hates ceremony.
SONYA. Someday I'll go with you to Indianapolis. I want to see what made you: your high school, where you first unsnapped a girl's bra— all the historic sites. They have Jews, right?
DAVID. In Indianapolis? Of course they do.
SONYA. I'm concerned about hate crimes.
DAVID. Who's going to know you're Jewish, anyway?
SONYA. Maybe I'll tell someone. Will they be shocked? Those Hoosiers?
DAVID. It's perfectly safe.
SONYA. *(Embracing him.)* I should be going with you, David; I know that. But phobias are real. If I had more notice I could've taken a bus.
DAVID. Don't worry about it. I understand. *(He kisses her.)*

(Two. Lights shift to DAVID, alone.)

DAVID. My mother always hated the suburbs. The gated communities, the cul-de-sacs named after Robin Hood and his Merry Men, the covenants about paint colors and what kind of bark you

THE SAFETY NET

can put in the flower bed— to her that's fascism. So even after my dad was pretty successful we didn't move. We had a little brick house with a porch where we used to keep our bikes and a detached garage. One car. It wasn't a bad neighborhood— Indianapolis doesn't really have bad neighborhoods. My parents' friends, of course, my father's colleagues, they all lived in the suburbs. But my mother thought it was important we rub elbows with people who weren't so fortunate. So I went to public school. My best friend's dad was a Roto Rooter guy. And even though my mother didn't really socialize with the neighbors, she did chat with them at Little League games and in the line at the supermarket and it made her feel good to think her son's upbringing was so much more "mixed" than hers had been. So naturally, when it came to adopting my little brother— which happened when she was pushing 40 and could no longer say with conviction that she'd finish her PhD— the one thing she told everybody about the adoption was that she absolutely did not care what color skin her baby had. *(Beat.)* I think it was a bit of a disappointment when Gene turned out to be white.

(Three. We hear faint party chatter as lights shift to DAVID's childhood bedroom in Indianapolis. A twin bed with a cardboard box on it. DAVID and RICK ENTER.)

RICK. I hope Carsey didn't see me come upstairs. It would be a major drag if she thought I was sneaking out on her. *(DAVID takes a flask of vodka and paper cups from his jacket pockets.)* She's definitely jonesing on me, you can see that, right? But she's got a kid so you don't want to go there. Even before I got married I had scruples not to be dealing with a kid the morning after— reading Power Rangers off the back of the cereal box and he wants to annihilate you because you porked his mom. You have to set higher standards than that.

THE SAFETY NET

DAVID. She must be a premium client.

RICK. She was half my commissions last year. I had no clue she's a friend of your family. *(DAVID hands him a drink.)* I've been dying for this. Who ever heard of a non-alcoholic funeral reception?

DAVID. Out of respect for my brother's problem.

RICK. Obviously. I'm borderline retarded— you knew that, right? It was a very nice service. Unusual.

DAVID. My mother didn't want a traditional thing.

RICK. People are more creative these days. Which I like.

DAVID. You make anything of his girlfriend?

RICK. The homegirl?

DAVID. LaShonda.

RICK. LaShonda— right. I knew it was something along those lines.

DAVID. Gene never mentioned her. Maybe he thought I'd be uncomfortable about him dating an African-American.

RICK. You're way too bleeding heart for that.

DAVID. You didn't have a take on her?

RICK. Not so much.

DAVID. It's interesting my parents let her spread some of the ashes. Which my father tells me aren't technically speaking ashes— they're actually pulverized bone fragments. *(Off RICK's look.)* His way of dealing was to read up on the cremation process.

RICK. That's different.

DAVID. I'm not sure what LaShonda was getting at in her remembrance.

RICK. Very moving, I thought.

DAVID. Well, yes. But I can't say I followed it, really. Apparently they were engaged?

RICK. Oh, yeah. The whole thing's tragic.

DAVID. I hope Gene didn't make any promises, you know, that she's expecting my parents to keep. Financially speaking.

THE SAFETY NET

RICK. You think she's after money?

DAVID. I just don't want my parents to suffer any more than they already have.

RICK. My heart goes out, man, what can I say? I mean, a car wreck? When you think how fucked up we used to get— and riding around with Marty Schimmel, who wasn't exactly AJ Foyt behind the wheel even when he was sober... It could've been us, right? Gene just had the destiny.

(Pause.)

DAVID. I really need to get back to New York. Whenever I'm home I start scratching messages in my skin like I'm some 14 year-old girl with an eating disorder.

RICK. That was your stroke of genius— getting out.

DAVID. The service didn't work for me, to tell the truth. I don't want to dwell on it, but there it is.

RICK. Well, it's more for your folks.

DAVID. Pulverized bone fragments— can you believe that? And my mother's reading Desiderata as if it was some favorite of Gene's, as if he read a poem since Dr. Seuss. And LaShonda's there blubbering— openly, sincerely, like some innocent child who stumbled into our psychotic family death pageant. When she first arrived I had no idea she was connected to Gene, of course, that she had a relationship with him. I assumed my mother hired her to sing "Amazing Grace" while we all joined hands in the circle of remembrance. Can't we just do a funeral? With a church and a minister and great aunts crying through their veils? At least you have some sense of ritual with that, some— some formality. This thing today was like a really lousy picnic. *(Beat.)* That was sort of an outburst.

RICK. Why don't you come over for dinner tomorrow? Joanie would love to see you.

THE SAFETY NET

DAVID. I have to get back. You should've seen the bitching and moaning over me taking two days.

RICK. I bet they crack the whip out there, don't they?

DAVID. I'm being reviewed for partnership.

RICK. You've got that locked up, I'm sure. *(DAVID shrugs.)* It's really great to see you, man— I get tired of the hicks. It's so hard to have ambition in this town. *(Points to himself.)* Corporate agent of the month in February. It's a short month so it's the most coveted. *(A beat. He finishes his drink.)* Well, I should probably get back downstairs and perform my due diligence on Carsey.

DAVID. You know where this is?

(Holds out a scrap of paper.)

RICK. That's in Stringtown.

DAVID. Stringtown?

RICK. Very urban. Gangs and shit.

DAVID. That's where LaShonda lives.

RICK. You're going to drop in?

DAVID. On my way to the airport maybe. Make sure she doesn't have any...expectations. Is it dangerous?

RICK. It's what I might call a coverage risk. But I'm sure it's safe in the morning. Crackheads probably sleep in.

DAVID. Gene was like a ten-year nightmare for my family, you know? I just want to be sure LaShonda doesn't prolong the agony.

RICK. Sure.

(TRUDY knocks and ENTERS.)

TRUDY. I thought you might be hiding in your room. Hello, Rick.

RICK. It's my fault, Mrs. Chandler. I led him astray like al-

THE SAFETY NET

ways.

TRUDY. *(Smiling.)* I won't argue with that. *(To DAVID.)* The reception is starting to break up, honey. People want to say goodbye to you.

DAVID. I'll be right down.

RICK. I was just leaving anyway.

TRUDY. I'm so glad you could come, Rick.

RICK. It was a lovely service, Mrs. Chandler, very moving.

TRUDY. Thank you.

RICK. Take it easy, David. I'll give you a buzz in a week or two.

DAVID. Take care.

(RICK EXITS. Pause.)

TRUDY. Are you all right?

DAVID. I'm fine.

TRUDY. We should get back to our guests.

DAVID. I'm just going to finish my drink first.

TRUDY. Were you looking for something in Gene's box?

DAVID. I think Dad left that in here.

TRUDY. Those are my treasures. Every picture he colored since kindergarten, every spelling test and mention in the school paper... Dad doesn't touch that box. He's not sentimental.

DAVID. He was moving things around, said he wants to turn Gene's room into an office.

TRUDY. You may look through it, if you like. Perhaps there's something you want for yourself.

DAVID. There used to be a file in there, right? The adoption records.

TRUDY. The records are in our safety deposit box at the bank.

DAVID. That makes sense. You know, Dad should do something with my room while he's at it— I don't really need my high school style preserved in amber.

TRUDY. Were you looking for the records?

DAVID. I was afraid they were lost.

TRUDY. Of course they're not lost, David.

DAVID. It's funny, I remember knowing where you kept the files but I don't think I ever bothered to read them.

TRUDY. We must've shown them to you at the time. I mean, you are the lawyer in the family.

DAVID. I was 10 when you signed them.

TRUDY. Even when you were 10 you had a remarkable mind. I remember when you were in third grade they told us you were already reading at a college level of comprehension.

DAVID. Community college, maybe.

TRUDY. Gene was about to make assistant manager at the copy store. And LaShonda isn't a bad person. I wish she didn't have those children at such a young age. The accident was so unfair, David. He was borderline, barely over the limit. The officer said drinking quite possibly wasn't the cause.

DAVID. He just lost control, could've happened to anyone. The road was slick.

TRUDY. At least no one else was hurt. Something to be thankful for.

DAVID. *(A beat.)* So Gene was doing better.

TRUDY. You hadn't talked to him lately?

DAVID. He doesn't have a phone.

TRUDY. He asked me how you were doing the other day. I got the impression he was going to call you.

DAVID. Not lately.

TRUDY. You can imagine how hard it was for him to call.

DAVID. I'm tough to reach sometimes.

TRUDY. I remember the first time he was arrested and I— my

THE SAFETY NET

God, I'd never seen the inside of a jail before in my life— I remember how sullen he looked, how rude he was with the policemen, cursing a streak— on dope, I'm sure of that. And I knew, so clearly I knew I could never understand him the way I understand you. Not because I didn't want to, but because he was such a different person, so far away. Someday, God willing, you'll have your own child and I just pray you never have that feeling, that feeling of not being able to recognize your own baby.

DAVID. *(A beat.)* I'm sorry, mom.

TRUDY. If you want the key to our safety deposit box, you should ask your father. If you think that's necessary.

DAVID. I don't need the key.

TRUDY. I thought you wanted to see the adoption records.

DAVID. I just wondered where they were. I have an early flight tomorrow so I wouldn't have time anyway.

(Pause.)

TRUDY. We should get back downstairs.

(Crosses to door.)

DAVID. I'm right behind you.

TRUDY. I bet you're doing some marvelous things at work these days. Your father and I want to hear all the details at dinner.

DAVID. The partners seem pleased with me.

TRUDY. I'm very grateful you could be here, David. I'm aware of the demands on you.

DAVID. Did you think I wouldn't come?

TRUDY. I'm just grateful, that's all.

DAVID. It was a lovely service.

THE SAFETY NET

(TRUDY holds the door open for him.)

(Four. Lights shift to the sidewalk near LASHONDA's house. She ENTERS, counting bus fare from her pocketbook. DAVID ENTERS.)

DAVID. LaShonda?
LASHONDA. Oh. Hi.
DAVID. I hope this isn't a bad time.
LASHONDA. David, right? Not Dave.
DAVID. Yes.
LASHONDA. *(Smiling.)* He said you smacked him if he called you Dave.
DAVID. A long time ago, maybe. Childish hijinks.
LASHONDA. You want his things or something?
DAVID. Did he leave me something?
LASHONDA. Not really.
DAVID. I just wanted to say goodbye. I was expecting to see you at the reception and then—
LASHONDA. My sitter let me down.
DAVID. My mother said you have children.
LASHONDA. Two boys. You don't—
DAVID. Not yet. Can I treat you to a cup of coffee or some other poison?
LASHONDA. I got my class. I was just leaving for the bus.
DAVID. I could drive you.
LASHONDA. To the bus stop?
DAVID. All the way, if you like.
LASHONDA. I don't want to put you to any trouble.
DAVID. Are you sure?
LASHONDA. I'm fine.
DAVID. I just wanted to stop by because, well, Gene and I

THE SAFETY NET

weren't that close lately but—

LASHONDA. Did you used to be? Close?

DAVID. When he went through his rehab, you know, he said a lot of things about me, about my parents— they told us it was part of the therapy. But some of what he said, it made it hard for us to talk after that.

LASHONDA. Because he told the truth?

DAVID. Well, the truth— that's sort of moot, isn't it? That's open for discussion.

LASHONDA. Not the truth about how he felt.

DAVID. I can't argue with his perceptions. But what actually happened might be—

LASHONDA. You talk like a lawyer.

DAVID. Well, I am a—

LASHONDA. I know. But I figured you'd be more smooth.

DAVID. I do immigration. Look, I don't want there to be any animosity between us, okay? At the memorial service it was obvious you cared for Gene. And I was touched by that and I just wanted to be sure he hadn't, well, led you to believe—

LASHONDA. Led me to believe what?

DAVID. My parents stopped supporting Gene years ago. It was a painful decision but it had to be done.

LASHONDA. He never promised me nothing. Especially not from his parents.

DAVID. That's good. Sometimes Gene had a habit of—

LASHONDA. He changed his name to Sharron.

DAVID. I'm sorry?

LASHONDA. People don't call him Gene anymore.

DAVID. Really? Sharron? When did he— legally, you mean?

LASHONDA. Couple years ago.

DAVID. Is that right?

LASHONDA. He told me he had a dream about his real mama.

THE SAFETY NET

In the dream he was called Sharron.
    DAVID. Well. As I said, we haven't been close.
    LASHONDA. Then I'm guessing he didn't tell you I'm pregnant neither.
    DAVID. *(A beat.)* No.
    LASHONDA. You don't know much, do you? You mind dropping me by the bus stop? Now I'm late.

(DAVID stares at her a moment, then nods.)

(Five. Lights shift to a B&B in Maine. Two Adirondack chairs. SONYA is looking at the sea as DAVID ENTERS with coffee.)

    DAVID. This is great, isn't it? They didn't have soymilk so I used non-dairy creamer.
    SONYA. I don't mind.
    DAVID. I also got one black, just in case.
    SONYA. All week, you know, looking forward to Maine, I forgot how utterly taken for granted I am at the network. Because— and this was my great insight of Thursday afternoon— because when you do public relations you spend all your time stroking people but no one ever strokes you. Right? It's like being a geisha, I think, or maybe not exactly. Anyway, this weekend is perfect because my husband knows exactly how to stroke me.
    DAVID. Well...
    SONYA. And I'm not just talking about smut. I'm also talking about trying so hard to get the right non-dairy product for my coffee and other things, tiny courtesies, of that sort. Are you really and truly not mad?
    DAVID. That you didn't go?
    SONYA. That I couldn't.
    DAVID. Of course not.

THE SAFETY NET

SONYA. I wish I could've been with you, David— met LaShonda and everything.

DAVID. You'd like her, I think.

SONYA. Going to see her was such a lovely gesture on your part. And not so much in character for you, which makes it even more meaningful.

DAVID. I don't want to pretend like I'm some kind of...

SONYA. Don't apologize.

DAVID. She and Gene were engaged, or pre-engaged, as she put it. Sharron, I mean.

SONYA. I don't believe he changed his name. Not legally.

DAVID. Maybe just in her community.

SONYA. He wasn't black, David. He was at our wedding, do you understand? Unless he had some kind of surgery—

DAVID. Surgery?

SONYA. If anything, he was sort of a redneck. He chewed tobacco at the reception.

DAVID. I remember he used to drive me crazy when he was little, spinning a 45 of "Rhinestone Cowboy" on his record player over and over.

SONYA. What's "Rhinestone Cowboy"?

DAVID. A Glen Campbell song.

SONYA. Is he black?

DAVID. Country and western.

SONYA. See what I mean? *(Beat.)* Not that it matters.

DAVID. What?

SONYA. Gene can be whatever he wants to be. He tanned easily, yes, but lots of people tan easily.

DAVID. I'm surprised my mother didn't say anything to me. It's not the sort of thing she'd be ashamed of.

SONYA. Maybe she didn't know.

DAVID. She knew about LaShonda.

THE SAFETY NET

SONYA. Is LaShonda pretty? I'm just asking.

DAVID. I don't know.

SONYA. Of course you know, David. I'm not trying to trap you. But you're taken with her, I can tell.

DAVID. Come on.

SONYA. I don't think it's sexual, I really don't, but you're rhapsodic when you speak of her.

DAVID. She's not what I expected, that's all. She's ambitious—taking courses, wants to be a dental assistant.

SONYA. Does she have children?

DAVID. Two. Her mother helps take care of them.

SONYA. She's on welfare, I assume.

DAVID. I've been thinking we should help her somehow.

SONYA. I'd like that.

DAVID. I don't want to give her money. That seems impersonal.

SONYA. What do you have in mind?

DAVID. I left some groceries for her. Is that ridiculous? I have no idea what she eats. So I went to the supermarket and just picked things, I don't know, a lot of breakfast cereal for the kids. Milk, bread. Basics. I remembered how Nick's son is allergic to peanut butter so I didn't get that just in case. But what if her kids love peanut butter?

SONYA. You weren't shopping for the rest of their lives.

DAVID. Of course. But I wanted to get the right things.

SONYA. You don't really know any poor people, do you?

DAVID. Do you?

SONYA. Not poor like on welfare, not to that extreme.

DAVID. I realize it's naive to think a bag of groceries is going to make much difference.

SONYA. It's nothing to be ashamed of.

DAVID. I'm not ashamed.

THE SAFETY NET

SONYA. I'm proud of you, David. I'll clean out my closet; I have piles of old clothes I never wear.
DAVID. I might go through Indianapolis on my way back from Chicago next week. Check in on her.
SONYA. Overnight?
DAVID. I can spend the weekend with my folks. With the service and everything, we didn't get much chance to talk.
SONYA. You're not going to get terribly involved.
DAVID. No. But I want to do more than just send a check.
SONYA. I know it's touch and go for you at work, being under review and everything.
DAVID. It's doable.
SONYA. I know.
DAVID. I'm just dropping off groceries, you know; I'm not turning into Mother Theresa.
SONYA. *(Rising.)* Well, I'm going to take a shower— no, a bath. A bath feels more like vacation.
DAVID. All right.
SONYA. What are her children like?
DAVID. I didn't meet them.
SONYA. Boys? Girls? Babies? Toddlers?
DAVID. I don't really know. Two boys, I think.
SONYA. Next time you're there, ask for a picture.
DAVID. A picture?
SONYA. Yes, David, lots of pictures. I bet they're adorable. *(She EXITS.)*

(Six. A pool of light comes up. DAVID crosses into it.)

DAVID. The first year after we got married Sonya took too many... Well, she attempted suicide. Fortunately she was clueless about dosages and things. She just took a bunch of these over-the-counter pills that the drug companies make incredibly weak so they won't get sued. But it scared me. When I got home she was in front of the TV and I couldn't wake her up and I saw the bottle and she'd vomited everywhere, in her sleep, all over her face, so I called 911 and waited with her, held her with my cheek next to hers so I could hear her breathing... Later in the ambulance I found myself praying for the first time in years. I was, of course, praying that Sonya be spared, but more than that, I guess, I was praying for some sort of guidance. I've never been good in a crisis. There's a certain level of emotional complexity that a situation can reach where I just say, you know, I'm not very good at this, perhaps I should step aside and let an expert handle it. I knew if Sonya woke up and told me something horrible— that she didn't love me anymore, that her father had molested her— the things that went through my mind... Whatever it was, you know, it seemed likely we'd have to work through it, that I'd have to be there for her, and as much as I wanted to be one of those people you can count on I just knew I'd pull away. It's so humiliating to admit that. *(Beat.)* Anyway, long story short, she woke up and I asked her: why, Sonya, why did you do this? She said she couldn't remember. She was watching TV, something gloomy on PBS, she was crying and after that it's all a blank. She had to spend some time in therapy, of course, but she's been fine ever since. The doctors say we'll probably never know what happened. It may be that a combination of hormones, what she'd eaten that night and the program on PBS produced an acute form of depression, chemistry beyond what science can explain. But to me it wasn't chemistry at all. I remembered my mother's favorite little saying— that God only gives us what we can handle. And God knows I couldn't handle it if Sonya were truly sick. I'm just not one of those people.

(Seven. Lights shift to LASHONDA's house. A ragged sofa. A TV murmurs as LASHONDA flips through a textbook. Then a tod-

THE SAFETY NET

dler wails, off. She looks toward the crying and counts softly to ten. The baby quiets. She goes back to reading. But then there's a knock at the door, off. She crosses toward it warily.)

LASHONDA. Who's there?
DAVID. *(Off.)* David Chandler. May I come in?

(LASHONDA EXITS.)

LASHONDA. *(Off.)* I thought you went home.
DAVID. *(Off.)* I did, but I came back to check on my parents. Your house is on the way from the airport.

(A beat. LASHONDA returns with DAVID. He is carrying two paper bags.)

LASHONDA. You shouldn't be coming around here at night.
DAVID. I just thought I'd drop these off.
LASHONDA. Groceries?
DAVID. My wife sent some clothes, too. I don't know about the sizes, but, you know, just keep what you want.
LASHONDA. You left that sack the day after the funeral, didn't you?
DAVID. That's right.
LASHONDA. I hope you don't think we're starving or something. I know this house looks like a junkyard but mama's on disability so we do all right.
DAVID. I was just trying to be friendly.
LASHONDA. You might want to stick by the window, make sure nobody messes with your car. *(DAVID peeks outside as she unpacks groceries.)* You paid too much for these pork chops.
DAVID. Do they eat peanut butter?

THE SAFETY NET

LASHONDA. Who doesn't? Next time you come calling at night, park up the street by the firehouse. Nobody's gonna mess with your car up there.

DAVID. How are you feeling? I mean with the baby and everything.

LASHONDA. I guess I'm pretty good.

DAVID. You know, if you're looking for an obstetrician I could ask my mother to call around— she's good at that sort of thing. We don't have to tell her what it's really about.

LASHONDA. You want to get me a doctor?

DAVID. If the best one doesn't take your coverage, I can, you know, help make up the difference.

LASHONDA. *(Skeptical.)* Really? 'Cause the other day it's like—

DAVID. I want to apologize for that. I made an assumption and it was, well, prejudiced, wasn't it?

LASHONDA. At least you admit it.

DAVID. When you told me about the baby it made me think. It's a very hard thing to do by yourself—

LASHONDA. I got my mama.

DAVID. Of course you do, but still, I think Gene would want me to help. Sharron. You and I are sort of— well, we are— family.

(Pause.)

LASHONDA. I was studying when you came by. Did I tell you I'm going to be a dental assistant? It's a rising career opportunity.

DAVID. I've read that.

LASHONDA. And if I keep going on it I can get the hygienist degree— they make like 30 dollars an hour. And you get to meet all kinds of people, too. You want me to check you out?

DAVID. My teeth?

THE SAFETY NET

LASHONDA. We're supposed to practice.
DAVID. Oh. Sure.

(Opens his mouth.)

LASHONDA. Move into the light a little. *(DAVID bends over awkwardly.)* Yeah, that's better. You use baking soda toothpaste? *(DAVID grunts no.)* You should. The foaming action makes you brush longer. You're looking good. You can close.
DAVID. How long does it take to get your degree?
LASHONDA. Two more terms if I pass coronal polishing. But I don't know if I'm gonna keep going on it. Takes me near an hour and a half on that stinky bus and that gets real old.
DAVID. I have a long commute, too. On the subway.
LASHONDA. Mama's always lecturing me, talking about how they got a time limit on the check now, how I gotta get a job before the check runs out. Which is okay, I got no problem with working, but riding that bus, that's a grind. *(Beat.)* It was my car Sharron smashed up.
DAVID. You didn't have insurance?
LASHONDA. You mean like Drunk-ass Nigger Insurance or something? *(Beat. Softer.)* I don't mean... That boy let me down. He told me he quit drinking.
DAVID. What if I talked to your caseworker— maybe she could help you find a new car.
LASHONDA. You think public assistance is gonna get me a car?
DAVID. I could look into it.
LASHONDA. *(Smiling.)* You go right on When Little Miss Skinny found out Sharron was living with me, she nearly took my check away. He had to have some blood test to prove he wasn't Marcus and Tunde's daddy.

THE SAFETY NET

DAVID. I don't how they can expect people to work if they don't have transportation. *(Takes out a pen and paper.)* What's your caseworker's name?

LASHONDA. Heather something. She has a nose ring.

DAVID. I'll call her Monday.

LASHONDA. Tell her I want a Pontiac— a red one. Or black. I don't want no funky colors— only fools and pimps be driving a purple car.

DAVID. *(Writing.)* Red or black...absolutely no purple...

LASHONDA. Are you for real gonna call her?

DAVID. Absolutely.

LASHONDA. Don't tell her I put you up to it.

DAVID. I'll be very slick. I'm a lawyer, you know. *(Pause.)* Well, my mother is expecting me. Would it be all right if I came by again?

LASHONDA. Okay.

DAVID. I'm here for the weekend. Maybe Sunday?

LASHONDA. I'll be around after church.

DAVID. Good. Well, I should go.

LASHONDA. It's late; I better walk you to your car.

(She leads DAVID to the door.)

(Eight. Lights shift to a waiting area. Two folding chairs. DAVID ENTERS and waits. Then DEB ENTERS with a file.)

DEB. Sorry we have to do this in the hall. I don't have a private office. Please sit down.

DAVID. Thank you.

DEB. Usually the only attorneys I see are from Legal Aid.

DAVID. It's pro bono.

DEB. I can't release much information without the birth mother's

THE SAFETY NET

consent.

DAVID. I'm planning to file a petition with the county.

DEB. Did they tell you how long that'll take?

DAVID. I understand there's a backlog.

DEB. Last time somebody tried a petition it took three years.

DAVID. You must know a quicker way.

DEB. Well, my office can contact her and ask if she's willing to unseal her file. We can probably have an answer for you in a couple of weeks.

DAVID. Wonderful. Everybody upstairs said you were the person to talk to.

DEB. Really? *(Offers DAVID a form.)* Just fill this out and have your client sign at the bottom.

DAVID. What can you tell me in the meantime?

DEB. From the file? Not much.

DAVID. Any family history of drug abuse or mental illness?

DEB. They didn't record that sort of thing back then.

DAVID. Race?

DEB. Is there some doubt in that area?

DAVID. Well, my client was told he was half-Puerto Rican but—

DEB. That's a new one.

DAVID. That's what his parents were told at the time.

DEB. We don't have a lot of Puerto Ricans in Greencastle. I mean, maybe the exception to prove the rule.

DAVID. I don't understand.

DEB. In those days the counselors might fudge a little on the race issue. It was harder to place the African-American babies and if you had a biracial kid, you know what I mean, light-skinned and everything, you might tell the parents Mexican or even Filipino instead of black. Simply because it made it easier to place the baby.

DAVID. My client's parents would've been happy to take an African-American child.

THE SAFETY NET

DEB. *(Confidentially.)* A lot of folks say that, then they get particular at crunch time.

DAVID. So you're saying he's black?

DEB. Biracial, yes, that's quite possible. I'm sure he didn't have two black parents— that'd be stretching it.

DAVID. But what does it say in there?

(DEB looks inside the file. Pause.)

DEB. "Mother white, father unknown." You take a white girl with a black boy's baby around this area— I mean, 25 years ago? You got a real good chance to get an adoption out of that.

DAVID. So you don't know.

DEB. I'm afraid not.

DAVID. That's why my client wants to contact his birth mother.

DEB. Who can blame him? Let's just pray she's willing.

DAVID. This sort of thing isn't going on anymore, is it? With the counselors...I don't want to use the word "misleading"...

DEB. Oh, I don't, personally, myself. And if I ever saw anybody I'd definitely put a stop to it. But they did it with the best intentions, you know. Sometimes these babies come through the door and it just breaks your heart because you know you're never going to— and if you can do the slightest thing that's going to get them with a good family, somebody who can keep 'em in school, et cetera...

DAVID. My client has a right to know where he came from.

DEB. He didn't get on with his adoptive family?

DAVID. He got along fine with them.

DEB. In abuse situations the adoptee begins to idealize his birth family. Of course the reality rarely lives up to the fantasy.

DAVID. There was no abuse. His adoptive family gave him every opportunity.

DEB. That's good to hear. Well, then, just have your client sign

THE SAFETY NET

that form and we'll be on our way.
 DAVID. Thank you, Deb. You've been very helpful.

(DEB EXITS.)

(Nine. Lights shift to DAVID's bedroom. RICK reclines on the bed. DAVID ENTERS with two beers. Beat.)

 DAVID. So what do you think?
 RICK. I have my thinking cap on.
 DAVID. I wouldn't ask, but—
 RICK. I don't usually hang in Stringtown.
 DAVID. You park by the fire station— apparently that's safe. I'm talking once a week here, it's not like—
 RICK. Once a week?
 DAVID. To check in.
 RICK. Are you okay and everything?
 DAVID. Look, she's pregnant.
 RICK. Pregnant as in your brother's... *(DAVID nods.)* Whoa.
 DAVID. Things are crazed at work so I can't be flying out every—
 RICK. You don't have to tell me about pressure.
 DAVID. I know that.
 RICK. In my small way I also deal with—
 DAVID. So you understand. I haven't told Sonya about the baby yet because— well, for a variety of reasons, but mostly because at her age every discussion of infants turns into a deadly minefield.
 RICK. You're talking to a guy who stepped on three mines. You know how Joanie told me about our first? She puts the strip on my pillow as she leaves for work. I'm still asleep, okay, and I wake up to this urine-stinking strip on my pillow. Do you get that?
 DAVID. She was afraid of your reaction.

THE SAFETY NET

RICK. But I was happy.

DAVID. Sonya doesn't mention it directly. But she talks about wanting more meaning in her life, about not being respected at work... It's code.

RICK. But you don't...?

DAVID. Not yet. There's a— a fertility issue.

RICK. Joanie and I were lucky that way. If you ever need a donor thing, you know, what's mine is yours. I don't even consider that a favor. I mean, jacking off? You're doing me a favor.

DAVID. The situation is, Sonya and I are not completely at ease with each other right now. I don't think we can just push forward with— with— Right?

RICK. You're having problems. That makes sense.

DAVID. I don't want to make it sound dire.

RICK. Just normal—

DAVID. Normal friction. Yes.

RICK. The thing about this black girl, can I ask a question?

DAVID. Anything.

RICK. I'm not your beard, am I?

DAVID. Come on.

RICK. Don't be offended. She's an attractive girl.

DAVID. She's my brother's girlfriend, like his widow almost— and she's pregnant for fuck's sake.

RICK. Yeah, of course— sometimes I don't know where my head is. Up my ass, apparently.

DAVID. On the wall at her place, you know, there's this article— this framed article I don't even remember— some item from the paper about when I made Law Review— apparently Gene saved that. Which surprised me. The last ten years I didn't know him at all.

RICK. So now you have to make sure his baby comes out in one piece.

THE SAFETY NET

DAVID. I don't want my parents to have to deal with it, you know? They've cleaned up enough of Gene's messes. *(Beat.)* Look, if you can't do me this favor, just—
RICK. You know I'll do it. I'd take a bullet.
DAVID. Thank you.
RICK. In Stringtown I probably will take a bullet.
DAVID. LaShonda is different.
RICK. Look, just be careful. You always had a thing, you know, about the other side of the fence.
DAVID. What?
RICK. I'm not saying there's anything wrong with it. But, okay, Sonya's Jewish, right? And most of high school you went with that Mormon girl and I know it wasn't because you were getting laid. And now LaShonda—
DAVID. Just forget it. I'll get somebody else.
RICK. Don't act like that, man. I'm happy to do it.
DAVID. I love my wife, all right?
RICK. I didn't mean to touch a nerve. *(Beat.)* Look, I gotta run. You doing anything tonight? Maybe I'll give Joanie a call and we can grab a bite.
DAVID. I'm meeting LaShonda for dinner.
RICK. *(A beat.)* That's cool.

(Hold on DAVID and RICK, then...)

(Ten. Lights shift to LaShonda's house. Jazz on the radio. LASHONDA is trying to light a candle. It won't light.)

LASHONDA. *(Striking another match.)* I got the shakes or something.
DAVID. *(Off.)* I'd be happy to—
LASHONDA. I got it. *(Finally lights candle.)* Okay, you can

THE SAFETY NET

come in now. *(DAVID ENTERS.)* Nice, huh? Sit, sit.

DAVID. *(Sitting.)* Thank you.

LASHONDA. We're having pizza, okay? I do these pizzas from the box, mix in some hamburger, onion, green pepper if I got one, comes out pretty good. You like pizza?

DAVID. Sounds great.

LASHONDA. Dumb question. Everybody likes pizza.

DAVID. My roommate in college didn't like pizza. Or beer. He was sort of an outcast.

LASHONDA. Beer neither?

DAVID. He only drank cheap champagne. The really sweet stuff.

LASHONDA. I used to like that kind but I don't drink a drop no more. Wine makes me trigger off. I'll go back to hanging with pipers if I start drinking and I don't want to get messed up again.

DAVID. *(A beat.)* Right.

LASHONDA. Damn. Now you think I'm a crack ho, don't cha?

DAVID. I don't.

LASHONDA. I gotta open my big mouth. I never did it for real, you know? Not everybody who picks up a pipe turns into a hard case, not like they make out on TV. I just needed the sparkle sometimes. It was Sharron set me right; he took my ass in hand.

DAVID. My brother helped you get off the drugs?

LASHONDA. Yeah. I gotta check the pizza. I hope you're hungry, 'cause I made a big one.

DAVID. We could go out, you know. I don't want to put you to any trouble.

LASHONDA. Can't get pizza like this at a restaurant. *(As she EXITS.)* You want a RC cola?

DAVID. Whatever you have is fine.

LASHONDA. *(Off.)* How 'bout my candle?

DAVID. Vanilla, right? It's very pretty.

LASHONDA. *(ENTERING.)* Sets a mood, huh? And this place

THE SAFETY NET

don't look too good in bright lights, let me tell you.

(She gives DAVID a cola and sits next to him on the sofa.)

DAVID. Thanks.
LASHONDA. Me and Sharron got this sofa junking. Can you believe somebody threw this out? There's a big cat stain on one arm, that's why we got it pushed up by the wall.
DAVID. It's remarkable what people throw away.
LASHONDA. You ever been junking?
DAVID. No.
LASHONDA. You go up to the right neighborhoods, it's amazing what all you find. That TV set— works just fine— somebody threw it out. Didn't have the remote, though, so Sharron wrote a letter to the company, said we got this TV and it didn't have no remote and they sent us one for free. Sharron used to get all kind of stuff that way. *(Laughs.)* You know what Sharron says when he feels like going junking? He say "LaShonda honey, let's go to the mall tonight." He just cracks me up sometimes.
DAVID. When I was a kid we used to wait behind one of these hamburger places. They only keep the food under the heat lamps a certain amount of time and if they can't sell it by then, they just toss it. So we'd hide in the bushes and wait till after the lunch rush and when they'd bring that big sack out we'd grab it and run.
LASHONDA. Were you poor then?
DAVID. No. I guess it was the excitement. We thought we were stealing.
LASHONDA. If they throw it out, it ain't stealing.
DAVID. I suppose so.
LASHONDA. I don't go junking for my kids. They get new toys for Christmas and birthdays— that's a law with me and Sharron.
DAVID. Were you together a long time?

THE SAFETY NET

LASHONDA. Three years, on and off. I started seeing him when I was about to have Tunde. I had some complications and he was so sweet to me.

DAVID. Complications?

LASHONDA. Bleeding. Scary. Doctor said if I have more babies he's gonna watch me like a hawk. This jazz-type music okay with you?

DAVID. It's nice.

LASHONDA. Sometimes when I'm talking to somebody I just like for music to be on the air, you know? Sets a mood. Sharron always be putting on that hip-hop and rap, which you gotta crank up or what's the point? But I don't like it really. Bunch of gangbangers grabbing themselves, talking about raping hos and popping each other. Stupid. You know what I'm saying? Sharron just trying to be cool, listening to all that. Making sure everybody knew he was a brother. He was jealous about you.

DAVID. I doubt that.

LASHONDA. Oh, yeah. He was proud of you, too, always bragging on your ass with his friends, how you a lawyer in New Jack and all. But, you know, he's making copies 40 hours a week, never got out of high school, couldn't even pass the damn GED—

DAVID. He could've passed that if he'd applied himself. I mean, he was never that interested in school, but he wasn't dumb.

(LASHONDA is crying.)

LASHONDA. Don't mind me.
DAVID. Are you all right?
LASHONDA. Sometimes I get confused or something. I'm just...
DAVID. What's the matter?
LASHONDA. I'm stupid.
DAVID. It's all right— you can tell me.

THE SAFETY NET

LASHONDA. I was pretending like this was a date.
DAVID. A date?
LASHONDA. I'm not trying to jump you or nothing. I just haven't, for a real long time, sat down and talked to somebody. The fools I used to go with got their octopus hands all over me the second they come over, know what I'm saying? I just thought this could be a date-type date, like on TV. The girl cooks up something nice, there's candles, jazz music— I feel really stupid.
DAVID. I'm flattered you went to all this trouble. I just feel like I should— when you say "date"—
LASHONDA. I meant like a junior high kind of date, where you don't do nothing. At least you don't wanna do nothing.

(Smiles.)

DAVID. Oh. Well...
LASHONDA. Just talking and such, that's what I was thinking. But then we got going on Sharron and, I don't know, I just miss him so bad. And I started to feel like I was running around on him, even though, like I said, I don't want to do nothing. I'm not making sense, am I?
DAVID. You really loved him.
LASHONDA. Big time. *(Beat.)* Don't you ever mess with me, okay? 'Cause that would not be right.
DAVID. I wouldn't— I'd never—
LASHONDA. Thank you. Thank you so much. *(Beat.)* Sometimes, you know, sometimes Sharron would hit me. Not like beat on me or nothing, but sometimes— a smack or something. I can get sorta loose at times, I got a loud mouth and I'd just go off, you know? A smack, maybe. And when I used to get wild, you know what I'm saying? I could be real hard to deal with. So he had his reasons. I didn't like it, though.

THE SAFETY NET

DAVID. He used to beat you?
LASHONDA. Just open-handed.
DAVID. When he was drinking, probably. I'm not making excuses.
LASHONDA. Mostly he was drinking. He got into fights and all when he was drinking. But this wasn't fighting or nothing. Just smacks, you know, when things got outta hand. He never beat on me— I ain't putting up with that. It wasn't my fault.
DAVID. Of course it wasn't.
LASHONDA. Sometimes I really miss him and sometimes I don't.
DAVID. That's normal, I think. I'm sure it is.
LASHONDA. I never told nobody about the smacks, but you're family, right?
DAVID. Yes. Yes, we are.

(LASHONDA hugs him.)

LASHONDA. Sometimes I just gotta talk to somebody. Mama would go crazy if I told her about it.

(The hug goes on a moment more. Then LASHONDA steps back.)

(Eleven. Lights shift to DAVID's bedroom. TRUDY sets a pile of folded clothes on the bed. As she turns to EXIT, DAVID ENTERS.)

TRUDY. You startled me.
DAVID. This is sort of late for you, isn't it? The early bird.
TRUDY. It's only eleven. You're the one who should be in bed. You have to get up so early for your flight. *(Beat.)* You were out with Rick?

THE SAFETY NET

DAVID. *(With a smile.)* I don't still have to report in, do I?

TRUDY. I'm just asking.

DAVID. I was driving around.

TRUDY. I washed your shirts and undershorts. I couldn't sleep.

DAVID. You don't have to do that.

TRUDY. Just saving Sonya the trouble.

DAVID. Sonya doesn't wash my underwear.

TRUDY. Well, she works, I understand.

DAVID. You ironed them.

TRUDY. I told you, I couldn't sleep. *(Pause.)* It was thoughtful of you to check in on your father and me so soon after. God knows you must be busy at work.

DAVID. Well, I'm trying to look busy. For the partnership committee.

TRUDY. What sort of case are you working on now?

DAVID. The usual stuff.

TRUDY. I'm interested.

DAVID. I'm trying to get this Hungarian cellist visa-ed so he can do a U.S. tour. Vogelstein. He's not really known over here. It should be routine but he has these drug convictions on his record. He says they were cooked up by the old Communist regime to discredit him, but INS goes crazy over anything with drugs.

TRUDY. Your work is fascinating.

DAVID. Honestly, mom, I just fill out forms and make sure the Fedex guy comes for them.

TRUDY. I'm sure that's not how Mr. Vogelstein thinks of you.

DAVID. He won't think of me at all unless I screw this up.

TRUDY. Is this how people are in New York, David? Always minimizing their accomplishments?

DAVID. You're right— I shouldn't do that. The truth is, I'm huge in New York.

TRUDY. You're very nearly a partner at an important law firm.

THE SAFETY NET

DAVID. The firm's pretty small, really—
TRUDY. You're impossible.
DAVID. —but it was the only one hard up enough to take me.
TRUDY. It hurts me when you talk like that.
DAVID. I'm just kidding.
TRUDY. Your father told me about the safety deposit box. And don't blame him for blabbing because when I set my mind to it I'm quite an inquisitor.
DAVID. I just wanted to look at the records. You said you didn't mind.
TRUDY. I don't mind.
DAVID. You said to ask dad.
TRUDY. Yes, I did. I think we're handling it pretty well, don't you? We've got our hobbies, our little projects. Gardening, your father's paddle tennis. Keeping busy is the key because when we dwell on things—
DAVID. If there's anything I can do...
TRUDY. I don't want you to worry about us. That's all.
DAVID. I'm not worried.
TRUDY. You weren't out with Rick tonight, were you?
DAVID. What difference does it make?
TRUDY. David, I understand how you feel. That night, when the police called, I'm ashamed to say I wasn't even upset. It wasn't the first time, not by a long shot. I thought it was just a matter of bail. But when we got there Gene was pinned inside the car, I could see his cheek resting on the window as if he'd pulled over for a nap, but the policemen were just milling around, nobody rushing to pry open the door, so I knew. All I could think was that I'd failed him. Not that I was going to miss him, which is what I wish I'd felt— but only that I had failed him so deeply.
DAVID. You really shouldn't worry about the records, Mom. Nothing's going to come of it.

THE SAFETY NET

TRUDY. We all failed him, David. But we just have to keep going, hold ourselves together, because that's all there is. Sonya is counting on you. So is Mr. Vogelstein, for that matter. Next time you want to see your decrepit old parents, give us a call and we'll come to New York. Your father's leg is much better now. He doesn't mind the walking.

DAVID. *(Nodding.)* You're absolutely right. You should come for Thanksgiving maybe. It's a nice time to be in the city.

TRUDY. I'd like that. It was very thoughtful of you to come, David.

DAVID. It's nothing.

TRUDY. No, it's not nothing; it's very thoughtful. When you get to be our age, having a child who worries about you is very comforting. You're a responsible young man.

(She kisses him and EXITS.)

(Twelve. Lights shift. DAVID is alone.)

DAVID. Gene used to call me from time to time after he got out of rehab. Not often, you know, only when he had an achievement to report: a new job, another month sober, a car he bought secondhand. Things he knew I'd approve of. When he was in trouble, I guess, when he was ashamed of himself, he called someone else. *(Beat.)* Not long after he found out he was adopted— he was maybe five— Gene went through this period where he was really alienated from my parents. For months he barely said a word to them. Every night at bedtime he screamed bloody murder and wouldn't go unless I was the one who tucked him in. And I'm sure I was grudging about it, but I did it, told him stories till he fell asleep— I remember passing off the whole plot of Star Wars as my own work. I was the one who checked the closet for monsters, made sure the nightlight was on, fetched another glass of water because he said he was "parched"— this word he'd picked up from Gunsmoke... I guess you could say we were close. But then there was high school, girlfriends, going away to college and I lost him. Just— whatever— lost. Until recently it never occurred to me how much I still thought of him— how much I still treated him like that five year-old who couldn't sleep without me holding his hand. *(Beat.)* But I really loved that little kid. We were close.

(Thirteen. Lights shift to DAVID and SONYA's apartment. DAVID ENTERS.)

SONYA. *(Off.)* David? Is that you?
DAVID. Who else has a key?
SONYA. *(ENTERING.)* Just checking. *(Kisses him.)* You're home early. What's the occasion?
DAVID. No occasion.
SONYA. Good day?
DAVID. Just, you know— normal.
SONYA. Not normal, really. Not if Melanie let you go before ten.
DAVID. I guess it is an occasion. Maybe I should have a drink to celebrate.
SONYA. I have a bottle of wine in there.
DAVID. Do we have anything grown up?
SONYA. There's some creme de menthe.
DAVID. I'll go out.

(Starts for the door.)

SONYA. Something happened today.
DAVID. Something good, I hope.
SONYA. The bank called. They couldn't reach you at work this

THE SAFETY NET

afternoon so they called me. LaShonda was trying to cash a check on your account— 3,000 dollars. They thought maybe she'd stolen your checkbook.

DAVID. *(A beat.)* What did you say?

SONYA. I said you don't lose things. Not your keys, not your scarf and certainly not your checkbook. So the check must be legitimate.

DAVID. I'm sorry. I forgot to tell you about that.

SONYA. I thought you didn't want to give her money.

DAVID. LaShonda needed a car to get to her school. Those classes are important for her.

SONYA. We can afford it, right? Three thousand is—

DAVID. You can't get a decent car for less than that.

SONYA. We can always borrow money from my parents if we need to.

DAVID. We don't need to borrow from your parents.

SONYA. We have debts, David. The apartment, credit cards—

DAVID. I'm not going to ask your father—

SONYA. Just until you make partner. They're happy to do it, as long as we don't tell them we're supporting a welfare queen.

DAVID. LaShonda's not a welfare queen. It's a hell of a lot harder for her to be a dental assistant than it was for me to be a lawyer or you to—

SONYA. God, you're so earnest all of a sudden. Can't I make a joke? I was kidding. *(Beat.)* My lunch group thinks she's scamming you.

DAVID. You told your friends about LaShonda?

SONYA. I didn't say I agree.

DAVID. Jesus.

SONYA. Donna thinks you're screwing her.

DAVID. That isn't even worthy—

SONYA. She said it's the Pygmalion complex.

DAVID. I'm not screwing her.

THE SAFETY NET

SONYA. I know that, David. I know you.
DAVID. Donna reads too many women's magazines.
SONYA. I needed to talk things through.
DAVID. LaShonda is not scamming me.
SONYA. I don't mind about the car, really. I just wish you'd told me about it.
DAVID. I know. This Vogelstein case has gotten very complicated.
SONYA. Is it serious?
DAVID. No. It's just making a lot of extra work for me.
SONYA. Look at it this way: After you make partner, this is exactly the kind of case you can dump on an associate.
DAVID. I need to go back to Indianapolis for a few days.
SONYA. Weren't you just there two weeks ago?
DAVID. Apparently LaShonda got high the other night— the first time in years.
SONYA. I'm sorry to hear that.
DAVID. She was devastated about flunking this exam and instead of going home afterwards she went to see some old friends, these girls she used to smoke with. They knew she just cashed her check and they gave her wine until she triggered off and bought drugs for everybody and yes, she got high. But she knows she screwed up.
SONYA. I don't think you should get involved.
DAVID. I have to. Rick was going to be keeping an eye on her but—
SONYA. I need to know what the limits are, David. I need to know how involved we're going to get.
DAVID. This isn't a situation where I can necessarily define that.
SONYA. What is it you think you're going to accomplish?
DAVID. I'm going to be an advocate for her. That's what I do.

THE SAFETY NET

SONYA. Is that going to get her off crack?
DAVID. She's not an addict. It was a slip.
SONYA. How do you know that?
DAVID. I know her; she's not like that.
SONYA. Look, I'm trying to be sympathetic, but if LaShonda wants to screw up her life—
DAVID. She's pregnant, Sonya; she's not just doing this to herself.

(Pause.)

SONYA. I see.
DAVID. I know I should've mentioned—
SONYA. Now I get it; now I understand why you're so obsessed with her. You think you're the father, don't you? Not the literal father, of course— you're not ready for that— but the ice-cream-and-cake, take-him-to-the-circus, weekend-and-holidays dad. Congratulations.
DAVID. If I'd known I was going to get so involved, I would have told you about the baby.
SONYA. Am I on a need-to-know basis, David? It must be wonderful for you, spending so much time with a fertile woman.
DAVID. That's exactly why I didn't want to bring it up.
SONYA. Because I'm so neurotic, so threatened by any woman who can have a child? The only thing that threatens me is that you're more concerned with her problems than ours. And we have plenty.
DAVID. I have a responsibility to Gene.
SONYA. We saw him one time in the four years I've known you!
DAVID. That's the point, Sonya; I barely knew him. Now he's left LaShonda pregnant, with no money, and I can't just—
SONYA. You know something, David? It would be better if you

were fucking her.

(She EXITS. Blackout.)

END OF ACT I

ACT II

(One. Lights rise on DAVID, alone.)

DAVID. Many times, you know, with no thought to my dignity, so overdeveloped in high school— and babysitting— maybe if you're getting paid— a girl, obviously, who likes kids, and you're getting paid pin money or whatever— but a guy? It's humiliating. And they dress it up like it's a step on the ladder to maturity. As if making sure the brat doesn't burn himself on the stove is some ancient rite of passage. "You're so good with your brother," she would say, and I was. If good means sitting him in front of the TV to watch some mindless, some incredibly violent and inappropriate programming, The "A-Team", say, or an R-rated thing on cable, which became, you know, which became my defining act of childcare. Here, Gene, a liter of Coke, a bag of chips, watch TV and don't bother me. And come to think of it, is this really so different from bonafide parenting, from my own parents in fact, who were, God bless them, incredibly busy with life? Anyway, it developed into a routine, as these things do, with Gene making himself sick on junk food and graphic bloodthirsty destruction and I'd be off with the Cermak girl playing cards. Strip poker, to be precise. She had her limits, naturally, no further than underwear, which she rationalized as being the same thing as if we went to the beach. I learned later, in those group therapy sessions that destroyed so many lives, that some nights, many times in fact, Gene was spying on us, enjoying what were probably his first

THE SAFETY NET

hard-ons for cause. For this I feel, from Gene at least, that I deserve, I don't know, gratitude? Fondness? How many seven-year-olds have the pleasure— I mean, please, warped him? Which is why I think it was so unfair to bring it up. In that room full of alcoholics, many of whom have severe problems, to bring up this ancient memory of my diddling Lisa Cermak— with tears, no less, because... Who knows because? Because it scared him? Because he was dissatisfied with my babysitting? Christ. And then my mother pipes in. "It's true," she says, "you never played with him." Like she'd just solved the riddle of the sphinx, the mystery of the boy who had such opportunity and ended up in rehab, in jail for boosting a car— maybe if I'd watched Mr. Rogers with him instead of following my natural desire to get in Lisa Cermak's panties, maybe this family hell could've been avoided and I wouldn't be sitting in a circle of drunks with tears streaming down my face. *(Pause.)* Gene used to keep the adoption decree in his dresser beneath his beloved Spiderman underpants. My parents gave it to him with great fanfare one Christmas, wrapped up like a gift in this big box with tinsel. They probably read somewhere that adopted children liked such things, that it gave them a sense of comfort, but I don't think it had that effect on Gene at all. Once that decree was given to him, he had the unshakeable sense it could be taken away.

(Two. Lights shift to the sidewalk near LASHONDA's house. She is on her hands and knees. DAVID ENTERS.)

DAVID. Did you lose something?
LASHONDA. Hey, David, what's up? *(She wobbles as she rises.)* Whoa, that shit came up on me.
DAVID. Are you all right?
LASHONDA. I'm real good. Just can't find my keys. You wanna see my new car? My cousin put a woofer in the trunk and now the

THE SAFETY NET

stereo rumbles.

DAVID. Rick said you had a problem with a test.

LASHONDA. There they are. *(Picks up keys.)* Yeah, I flunked up coronal polishing— kept jamming the girl in the gums, can't be doing that. I hope you didn't come all this way over some old test.

DAVID. Why don't we get some coffee?

LASHONDA. I'm going up to class. Can I give you a ride someplace?

DAVID. You shouldn't—

LASHONDA. What?

DAVID. Drive, all right? You've been drinking.

LASHONDA. You can tell? Not that much.

DAVID. Rick tells me you and your friends—

LASHONDA. That was so stupid, okay? But I never would've told him if I was gonna touch a pipe again. I told Rick so he'd help me be strong. You're mad, aren't you?

DAVID. I'm not here to lecture you, but drugs, you know—

LASHONDA. It was only one time.

DAVID. —when you're pregnant—

LASHONDA. I know you're right. I ain't saying shit back to you right now, you see that?

DAVID. Yes.

LASHONDA. And I told Keisha and Marie and those other pipers to clear their asses off. I got my retest coming up and how am I supposed to study, you know? I am trying to better myself— I don't need their tragedy going on.

DAVID. I wish you would've told me this yourself.

LASHONDA. I let you down.

DAVID. Not me, LaShonda.

LASHONDA. Yeah, my own self. I'm stupid.

DAVID. You're not stupid.

LASHONDA. I just had a beer this morning 'cause of nerves,

you know? I haven't been to class since the test.

DAVID. Has Rick been checking on you at all?

LASHONDA. He's here every day almost.

DAVID. Every day?

LASHONDA. Just about.

DAVID. He hasn't— I mean, he hasn't done anything inappropriate, has he?

LASHONDA. Like try to jump my ass?

DAVID. Well—

LASHONDA. No. He just plays with my kids. Chills out.

DAVID. Good. Good. He got that insurance for your car, right?

LASHONDA. Oh, yeah. He signed me up at his friend's address so I'd get a better rate.

DAVID. *(A beat.)* I've been thinking a lot since you told me about how Sharron used to treat you— the hitting, I mean— I was really honored that you would share that with me. But, LaShonda, you know the drinking needs to stop.

LASHONDA. You don't have to tell me that. I won't drink no more, swear to God on 20 Bibles.

DAVID. It's just so important we take care of that baby.

LASHONDA. I know.

DAVID. Even just a few drinks can cause brain damage, behavioral problems— it's scary. And if you need help, I can— *(Sees LASHONDA is crying.)* What's the matter?

LASHONDA. I have to get to class.

DAVID. Did I say something wrong? What did I say?

LASHONDA. No, you said everything right— everything. I'm just late, that's all.

DAVID. If you need somebody to talk to, I'm going to be over at my parents' house for a few days.

LASHONDA. *(Hugging him.)* I got it under control.

DAVID. I know.

THE SAFETY NET

LASHONDA. You smell good.

DAVID. Thank you.

LASHONDA. *(Breaking off the hug.)* I gotta get over to my class.

DAVID. Let me drive you then. You really shouldn't drive.

LASHONDA. Can we go in my car?

DAVID. Of course. *(They start off.)* Is your mother going to be home later? Because the phone guy is coming to connect you.

LASHONDA. She's always here. She got asthma.

DAVID. This is my cell phone number. If anything comes up, just call me.

LASHONDA. You gave me this already.

DAVID. Did I? *(They EXIT.)*

(Three. Lights shift to DAVID's bedroom. RICK skims a high school yearbook. DAVID ENTERS with a familiar cardboard box.)

RICK. We better take that stuff over to Shonda's before she leaves to pick up Marcus. Her mother doesn't get me.

DAVID. You don't have to come. I mean, if you have other plans.

RICK. I don't mind.

DAVID. What are you looking at?

RICK. Senior yearbook. Your room is like a time machine. You don't mind if I skim your dedications, do you?

DAVID. Knock yourself out.

(He rummages in the box.)

RICK. Check out this page, man. Scored...scored...two yard line...would have, but didn't bring the condom... Oh, and Tanya Mears. She was awesome. Actually, the M's in general were very good to me. Looking for something in particular?

DAVID. My mom keeps all of Gene's crap in here. I thought I'd give some to LaShonda. She was pretty upset this morning.

RICK. She said you kinda freaked her out.

DAVID. What?

RICK. I got the impression you were a little harsh with her.

DAVID. She said that?

RICK. In so many words.

DAVID. She was drunk.

RICK. She told me.

DAVID. I wasn't harsh with her.

RICK. She can be sensitive.

DAVID. Should I pretend she isn't drunk? When did she call you?

RICK. I dropped by on my lunch break.

DAVID. And this just came up?

RICK. She brought it up.

DAVID. She asked you to talk to me.

RICK. I guess. It's no big deal. Just take it easy on her, all right? Giving her lectures about birth defects and shit. She's got two kids already, man. She knows.

DAVID. Apparently she doesn't.

RICK. Yeah, I'm not a licensed counselor.

DAVID. I'm not saying it's your fault. I mean, I understand she's got problems; she's under a lot of pressure. You know, my brother used to beat her.

RICK. Open-handed. She told me all about it.

DAVID. *(A beat.)* I'm going to stick around a little longer this time, make sure LaShonda sees a doctor.

RICK. That's a good idea. Just—

DAVID. What?

RICK. I don't know. Be cool about it.

THE SAFETY NET

DAVID. Right. Obviously.

RICK. *(Looking at yearbook.)* I wonder what they look like now.

DAVID. You don't think I buy that, do you? That you slept with all those girls?

RICK. Don't be jealous. It's years ago.

DAVID. Come on, you're 35 years old and you're going to lie to me about the girls you screwed in high school?

RICK. I'm not lying.

DAVID. Tanya Mears wouldn't have crossed the hall to spit in your locker.

RICK. That's extreme.

DAVID. No fucking way. Tanya Mears.

RICK. Look, I'm not saying it was a relationship.

DAVID. Listen to me. If you so much as bumped her tits in the hallway her boyfriend would've decapitated you. I would be visiting your grave.

RICK. What's with you?

DAVID. Nothing. I just think it's pathetic at this stage of our lives to be making stuff up.

RICK. You don't have to believe me.

DAVID. It's not a question of belief. You're lying. I don't even think you got laid in high school. Ever.

RICK. Okay, man, whatever. Let's just go to Shonda's.

DAVID. I think maybe I should go by myself this time. I mean, I'm going to give her these personal things, family things.

RICK. Why are you pissed at me?

DAVID. I'm not. I really appreciate what you've been doing here.

RICK. Look, David, I like going down there. Half of the time, I take my son— he plays with Shonda's kids. It's good for him to see how other people live, you know?

THE SAFETY NET

(TRUDY knocks and ENTERS.)

TRUDY. Sorry to interrupt. Hi, Rick.
RICK. What's up, Mrs. Chandler?
TRUDY. Is everything all right?
DAVID. We were on our way out.
TRUDY. David, honey, there's someone from your office on the phone.
DAVID. They called here?
TRUDY. He said your cell phone must be turned off. It sounds urgent.
DAVID. I'm sure it isn't.

(Pause.)

TRUDY. He's holding for you.

(DAVID EXITS.)

(Four. Lights shift to a waiting area. DAVID is sitting on one of the folding chairs. DEB ENTERS, holding a file.)

DEB. I'm afraid I have bad news.
DAVID. I see.
DEB. The birth mother has requested no contact.
DAVID. What's the next step?
DEB. Well, there isn't one, really. You can go ahead with a petition but they're hardly ever granted.
DAVID. I don't have three years, Deb.
DEB. I shouldn't say this, but it's for the best, really. Half the time these reunions end up a disappointment.
DAVID. My client is expecting a child.

THE SAFETY NET

DEB. Is he worried about hereditary diseases? It's usually easier to get the medical records unsealed.

DAVID. What I'm looking for isn't going to show up in a chart. I need to speak with the mother.

DEB. Were you intending to meet the mother yourself?

DAVID. On behalf of my client.

DEB. Usually it's the child who—

DAVID. My client doesn't want a reunion. He had parents. What he wants to know is whether certain behaviors that have troubled him, addictions— I can't really go into detail— but perhaps the mother can give him some kind of idea.

DEB. Well, I can't tell you anything from her file but, just as a general matter, the answer is probably yes.

DAVID. Yes to what?

DEB. She was probably troubled, too.

DAVID. I need something a little more specific than that.

DEB. Of course you do, I just...

DAVID. The last thing my client needs is to have his own child go through the hell he did.

DEB. I understand. I really do. I don't make these rules.

(DAVID gets out a sheaf of papers.)

DAVID. This is a database search I ran that covers all the births in this county at the time my client was born. I've been able to narrow it down to fourteen women who had boys. I guess we can be pretty sure he was one of them.

DEB. *(A beat.)* I guess we can.

DAVID. Now I could track down all fourteen women— I'm prepared to hire a detective. But for thirteen of them I'll just be wasting everybody's time.

DEB. Your client has good representation.

DAVID. Thank you.

DEB. It takes a long time to go through all those records. I know that as well as anybody.

DAVID. All I'm asking you to do is take a look at this list. When you see the right name, just let your eyes linger on it a moment. No words have to be spoken.

DEB. I can't do that.

DAVID. I understand. It's the system that's put us in this position. But what is my client supposed to do?

DEB. I'm sorry. If anybody ever found out...

DAVID. I don't think this basement is bugged.

DEB. I took an oath.

DAVID. *(A beat.)* The things you told me before, about the agency misleading parents, the lying about race... I hate to say it but that could be grounds for a lawsuit.

DEB. *(A beat.)* I have to get back to work.

DAVID. If anyone asks, I'll say I got the name from a database search and used a detective to track her down. You won't be mentioned. Whatever my faults, Deb, I'm a man of my word.

DEB. Excuse me. *(She EXITS.)*

(Five. Lights shift to a shopping mall food court in Indianapolis. LASHONDA and SONYA sit at a table. LASHONDA eats. Pause.)

SONYA. Well, you're very pretty.

LASHONDA. Nothing's going on between me and your husband.

SONYA. *(Laughing.)* Of course not. That isn't why I asked you to have lunch.

LASHONDA. I kinda thought it was.

SONYA. I just wanted to meet you, after hearing so many wonderful things. Do you think I'm pretty, too? For God's sake, don't

THE SAFETY NET

answer that. Sometimes my mouth works before my brain.

LASHONDA. You shouldn't tie your hair back like that. It's librarian-looking.

(Eats.)

SONYA. *(A beat.)* You're so lucky to be able to eat.

LASHONDA. I love tacos.

SONYA. Being pregnant just makes you eat like crazy, doesn't it?

LASHONDA. I guess. Don't you want your taco?

SONYA. My stomach is sort of clenched. I don't generally fly— it's a phobia not a handicap and I deal with it. You have two boys already?

LASHONDA. Yeah.

SONYA. That must be quite a burden.

LASHONDA. Mama does a lot of it. I'm at the dental academy most days, getting my certificate.

SONYA. I can't imagine letting my mother raise any more children. You two must have a good relationship.

LASHONDA. She's my mama. David's been so sweet to me, you know? Without that car I might've quit school.

SONYA. My husband is unusually considerate, isn't he?

LASHONDA. He's been good to me.

SONYA. If I did have a child I can't fathom not being there every second. Those early years are crucial.

LASHONDA. Mama's pretty good with them.

SONYA. I'm sure she is. What do I know about it, anyway? I don't have a baby. I imagine everybody goes into it with certain ideals, certain principles they think are sacred, and then the reality of it— the diapers, the screaming—

LASHONDA. They scream like you can't believe sometimes,

drive me up the walls. When you get really jacked up you gotta take ten, count up to ten.

SONYA. It might very well be that I'd just be overwhelmed by it all. Two weeks of nurturing and I might be begging David to hire a nanny. Because there's no way to know your temperament until it's tested. I might be one of those horrible mothers who suffocates her children and blames it on crib death.

LASHONDA. I saw her on TV.

SONYA. Well, I'm sure I'm not. I think I've reached the stage where if I had feelings like that I'd know to seek help. But the point is, as much as I think I'd be one of those fresh-faced mommies who always have their kids doing crafts and going to the zoo, always so clean and dressed in those perky clothes, maybe I wouldn't. That's all. One of these days I guess I'll just have to find out.

LASHONDA. Don't worry about it. You got a couple years left.

SONYA. Actually, I had endometriosis, which is God's little way of saying He hates your womb.

LASHONDA. For real?

SONYA. Yes. And now everyone I know is pregnant.

LASHONDA. You can still adopt, though.

SONYA. David has issues about adoption. I wish we'd known you and Sharron better.

LASHONDA. Sharron liked you— he said you're crazy.

SONYA. I'm a little over-sensitive, but it doesn't approach crazy, at least not by my definition. I only ever saw him at the wedding. May we speak in confidence for a moment?

LASHONDA. Okay.

SONYA. I do public relations for Taffyworks— the cartoon network?

LASHONDA. My boys watch that all the time.

SONYA. I can send you some premiums. A lot of my job, you see, is telling reporters that the sick and twisted acts of cartoon char-

THE SAFETY NET

acters are not in any way connected with the sick and twisted acts of small children in the Midwest who watch our network and then set fire to one another. And what frightens me isn't that I'm able to do this in the first place but that I'm actually starting to persuade myself. So I've been thinking I should find something more humanity-affirming, I guess. And each time I range over the question I always come back to mothering. The purity of that, I guess, and there's also a part of me that wants to know at least one child in the world isn't consuming the dreck on our network. You're so lucky, do you know that? To have children.

LASHONDA. They're real special.

SONYA. I want you to know that regardless of my flaky behavior today, which has to do with medication I took so I could get on the airplane, I have it in me to be a spectacular mom.

LASHONDA. I can tell you're gonna try real hard.

SONYA. And David— you know David— he'd be a very committed father, don't you think?

LASHONDA. Sure.

SONYA. I just want you to know that David and I are ready to be there for your child.

LASHONDA. Are you wanting to adopt mine and Sharron's baby?

SONYA. No— I would never ask you that. Never. That's just too sacred.

LASHONDA. Did David tell you to call on me?

SONYA. Oh, God, no. David would murder me if he knew I was talking to you. Please don't be offended. Believe me, I came here with the best intentions.

LASHONDA. I don't know if this baby's gonna make it. Doctor says he's real small for how far along I am. Might be a complication or something.

SONYA. How far along—

THE SAFETY NET

LASHONDA. About five months, I guess. I don't show much, do I?

SONYA. Maybe you should see a specialist.

LASHONDA. I just think maybe God will decide. I had some bleeding and when it gets to that, you know, it's not up to me anymore.

SONYA. That's very serious. If it's about the money—

LASHONDA. Sometimes I think it might be best if God did take him. I might let everybody down again— you know what I'm saying?

SONYA. You don't want the baby?

LASHONDA. I just want what's best. If I end up losing him or something it might just be God's will.

(Pause.)

SONYA. Well, if there's anything we can do...

LASHONDA. You can buy me some pantyhose on our way out.

SONYA. Pantyhose?

LASHONDA. My counselor set me up some interviews with dentists and all the hose I got are ratty-ass.

SONYA. I'd be happy to.

LASHONDA. I sure do appreciate it. *(She eats.)*

(Six. Lights shift to DAVID's childhood bedroom. TRUDY ENTERS with towels and extra pillows. DAVID and SONYA follow.)

TRUDY. This bed is so small. I wish you'd take ours.

SONYA. We'll be fine. It's cozy.

TRUDY. I often sleep in this room, anyway; David's father snores.

SONYA. Really. I wouldn't dream of it.

THE SAFETY NET

DAVID. Don't make a fuss, mom.

TRUDY. Well, of course I'm going to make a fuss. Sonya, it's a pleasure having you here at last. Tomorrow night we'd like to take you both out to our favorite restaurant.

SONYA. That sounds lovely.

TRUDY. And show you around Indianapolis a bit. It's not New York, I understand that, but we have our points of interest. I hope you like Italian food. That's what the restaurant is.

SONYA. I love Italian.

TRUDY. I should invite some friends to join us— show you two off.

DAVID. Don't do that.

TRUDY. *(Ignoring him.)* I can't believe you're going to share this bed.

DAVID. It's fine, mom. Really.

TRUDY. Don't say I didn't offer. *(Kisses Sonya on the cheek.)* Thank you so much for coming, Sonya. It's good you can be with David right now.

SONYA. I'm happy to be here.

TRUDY. Good night, David. Don't forget to call your office in the morning. The young man was very insistent.

DAVID. I won't.

(TRUDY EXITS. Pause.)

SONYA. So what do you have on your sheets? Football helmets? Soldiers? You probably wet this mattress a few times, didn't you? *(Lies on the bed.)* Oh, yeah, I could get to like this. Something about being in your old room makes me horny. *(Beat.)* What?

DAVID. Why are you here, Sonya?

SONYA. I told you.

DAVID. You don't fly. You don't ever fly.

THE SAFETY NET

SONYA. I missed you.

DAVID. Do you think I'm sleeping with her?

SONYA. No.

DAVID. Ever since your surgery you've been completely irrational about other women. I don't care about having a baby.

SONYA. That's the problem, David; I want you to care.

DAVID. Don't twist my words; you know what I meant.

SONYA. I just had to be my own judge of character. I bought her some pantyhose and we parted friends.

DAVID. Pantyhose?

SONYA. It's what she asked for.

DAVID. And that's why you came? Just to meet her.

SONYA. To be perfectly honest, part of me wasn't even sure she was real. I mean, maybe you had a lot of gambling debts and she was your cover story.

DAVID. LaShonda is very upset.

SONYA. About what?

DAVID. I don't know. When I called, she wouldn't come to the phone. What did you say to her?

SONYA. I don't remember precisely. Nothing.

DAVID. Did you tell her something about me? About Gene?

SONYA. David, I have to be honest with you. I'm not sure she's really pregnant. I mean, she doesn't show. There could be a variety of explanations but generally at five months you'd expect—

DAVID. She's not pregnant?

SONYA. Every time the baby was mentioned she got very weird, like she didn't want to talk about it. That's not normal.

DAVID. Why would she lie?

SONYA. She got control top, all right? Do you think a pregnant woman's going to get control top? I don't even blame her, David; she needs help. And you stumble into her life, well-meaning, grieving over your brother, but you just stopped by to say hello— to pay

THE SAFETY NET

respects, a formality. If she didn't tell you she was having Gene's kid, would you have gone back there? Would you have turned your life upside down? Bought her a fucking car? We don't have a car, for Christ's sake. But if she's pregnant all of a sudden you can't ignore her— she's family. Isn't that obvious?

DAVID. Is that what you said to her?

SONYA. No— of course not. She thinks we want to adopt her baby.

DAVID. What?

SONYA. I took a Percocet so I could make it through the flight and you know how I get— everything that comes into my head— blah— right out my mouth. She misunderstood me.

DAVID. So now she thinks what I've been doing here— she thinks it's some sort of bribe?

SONYA. I was only trying to tell her how much I like children.

DAVID. I don't want to adopt her baby.

SONYA. I know that.

DAVID. Do you have any idea how difficult it was to gain her trust? My brother used to beat her, for God's sake.

SONYA. How do you know he hit her?

DAVID. She told me.

SONYA. Exactly.

DAVID. It was very hard for her to say.

SONYA. By which you mean she cried?

DAVID. Don't be condescending.

SONYA. You're too smart to be taken in by this.

DAVID. She wouldn't come to the phone.

SONYA. Please, David, you need to come home. You came here with the best intentions but you're being manipulated.

DAVID. That's not true. God, Sonya, why did you come? You don't fly.

THE SAFETY NET

(He heads for the door.)

SONYA. Where are you going?
DAVID. I have to get out of here.
SONYA. David, where are you going? *(He EXITS. She follows him to the door, trying to keep her voice down.)* David— wait. I came out here to be with you. David. *(She EXITS after him.)*

(Seven. Lights shift to LASHONDA's house. She sits between RICK and DAVID on the sofa. A TV murmurs. LASHONDA pours herself wine.)

LASHONDA. Anybody gonna join me?
DAVID. Maybe you should slow down.
RICK. Why don't we go out? Get some Chinese food.
LASHONDA. That shit gives me headaches.
RICK. MSG?
DAVID. Sonya gets that too.
LASHONDA. I'll bet.
DAVID. Is anybody watching this?
LASHONDA. I got it in the corner of my eye. Might be something good coming on later and I don't want to miss it.
RICK. We could order a pizza.
LASHONDA. I'm not hungry myself, but I can make us a pizza from a kit. Tell Rick about my kit pizzas; I never made him one.
DAVID. Just slow down a little, all right?
LASHONDA. You better clear off before mama gets back from the doctor. She can take your hide right off.
DAVID. I'd be happy to explain things to your mother.
LASHONDA. That's what you think.
RICK. We really should eat something. If you feel like making a pizza or—

THE SAFETY NET

LASHONDA. Sharron see me drinking wine he'd be smacking me upside the head right now. I even look at a piper he'd be whipping me with a belt. But you got too much cool to be acting like that, huh, David? That's why you're famous.

DAVID. Famous?

LASHONDA. You been in the paper a buncha times. We got the clippings on the wall, don't we?

(Refills glass.)

RICK. Ease off a little, Shonda.

LASHONDA. Oh, I'm okay. I guess I can drink some wine in my own motherfucking house. I don't say it's good wine but I guess I can drink it.

DAVID. We need to talk about the baby.

LASHONDA. First time I saw her I knew she was your wife. I mean, I knew she was gonna be your wife before I saw her but even if I hadn't I woulda known. Y'all dress just alike. You wear her bras and shit? I'm not judging.

DAVID. Sonya was wrong. I'm not trying to defend her.

LASHONDA. Don't you have no influence on your woman? She got up in my ass, David— asking can she have my baby. You gotta slap some restraint on her.

DAVID. I didn't even know she was coming.

LASHONDA. Don't y'all communicate? Maybe she's got ideas there's something going on with us. And you know I would never let that happen. *(Beat.)* Did you tell her you're messing with me?

DAVID. Of course not.

LASHONDA. Maybe she gets off on that warped shit, I don't know. Are y'all swingers?

DAVID. You need to see a specialist as soon as possible.

LASHONDA. Don't be flipping the subject on me.

THE SAFETY NET

DAVID. This is the subject.
LASHONDA. I don't need no doctor. I got a doctor.
RICK. This guy's better than your clinic doctor, Shonda.
LASHONDA. I don't need no favors from him.
RICK. What if I pay for it?
LASHONDA. He's gonna want amnio and I hate those needles.
DAVID. You're worried about a needle?
LASHONDA. You ain't getting my baby. Especially she ain't.
DAVID. Sonya was confused; you have to understand.
LASHONDA. I don't have to do nothing. She got in my business. And no amount of pantyhose can change that.
DAVID. If I'd known she was going to come I would've—
LASHONDA. Don't lie to me, David! You think a fly phobic bitch is gonna get on an airplane just to have a taco with me? Acknowledge you put her up to it.
DAVID. Sonya had the idea we were involved, yes— that's why she got on the plane—
LASHONDA. You stabbed me in the back, David. And now you're gonna sit there all peppermint cool and tell me you didn't?
DAVID. I'm sure it had nothing to do with the baby at first but it all got twisted in her mind— she's been distraught lately— and it came out wrong.
LASHONDA. You're not right. Sharron told me years ago about how you all shifty like snake eyes, never talk straight— how you went to his rehab and stabbed him in the back— told him flat out in front of all those people that you wished your family never adopted him in the first place—

(Suddenly DAVID slaps her. A beat.)

DAVID. I'm—
LASHONDA. Damn.

THE SAFETY NET

DAVID. I'm sorry. God, I'm so sorry.

(Pause.)

LASHONDA. *(Softly.)* No, that's all right...sometimes I, you know, kinda run off at the mouth—
DAVID. Don't say that; don't tell me it's all right.
LASHONDA. I gotta be sick.

(EXITS.)

DAVID. *(A beat.)* I can't even believe... I don't know what happened.
RICK. You better leave.
DAVID. Yes— of course— I should go. Can you keep an eye on her?
RICK. She'll be okay.
DAVID. Just stay till her mother gets back.
RICK. Sure.
DAVID. I'll just come by in the morning, when she's sober.
RICK. I don't think you should come back for awhile.
DAVID. What, because I... She'll forgive me. Christ.
RICK. I know you mean well, but being here, hanging around so much, you're not helping.
DAVID. Not at the moment, obviously, but—
RICK. Maybe you should go back to New York.
DAVID. I've gone significantly out of my way to help her, you know? I've got this case that's falling apart and I'm not even taking the call— I'm up for partner this year— and Sonya—
RICK. I know.
DAVID. And then this? I mean, LaShonda doesn't seem to have any— any gratitude for what I'm trying to do here.

THE SAFETY NET

RICK. Is that what you want from her, David? Gratitude? Donate some money to the YMCA for fuck's sake— they'll send you a very grateful letter, suitable for framing.

(Pause.)

DAVID. I would never hurt her— you know that, right?
RICK. I know. Go home, David. Just go home.

(A beat. DAVID EXITS.)

(Eight. Lights shift to DAVID's childhood bedroom. He sits on the bed. SONYA ENTERS.)

SONYA. Sweetheart, the Rosens are here.
DAVID. I saw.
SONYA. Why don't you come down and say hello? Your mother's serving cocktails. Then we're going out for Italian, remember?
DAVID. That's good.
SONYA. It doesn't look so good when you hide in your room.
DAVID. I'll come down later.
SONYA. Is everything all right with LaShonda?
DAVID. Yes.
SONYA. You were there a long time.

(Pause.)

DAVID. I know this isn't your fault, Sonya.
SONYA. Thank you.
DAVID. I'm out of my element with LaShonda, I understand that, and I've put you in an impossible situation. So I know what-

THE SAFETY NET

ever you said to her came out of confusion and...being upset...

(SONYA sits next to him.)

SONYA. It's okay. You were trying to do something for your brother.
DAVID. I realize I can't go on the way I have been. *(Pause.)* I've been thinking about taking a leave from the firm and living here for a few months.
SONYA. Here?
DAVID. Until LaShonda's baby is born.
SONYA. Honey, if you take a leave now you'll never make partner.
DAVID. No, I've been thinking about that. If I tell them I have a substance abuse problem, you know, they have to give me a leave. They got sued by an associate a few years ago and now they bend over backwards if you mention rehab.
SONYA. Are you serious?
DAVID. I don't know; it's an option. As long as I complete the aftercare program, they can't hold my history against me when I come up for partnership again.
SONYA. Why not just make partner first? You're almost there. Then if you're still unhappy you can take a leave.
DAVID. The baby isn't going to wait for me.
SONYA. I think you should talk to someone.
DAVID. I've thought about this a lot.
SONYA. I don't understand what's happening to you.
DAVID. At first I thought I could do this from a distance, but a person with the kind of problems LaShonda has needs full-time attention.
SONYA. I'm really tired of LaShonda's problems.
DAVID. I know.

THE SAFETY NET

SONYA. She's so vulnerable, so poor and everything, so black. How can I compete with that? I just hate her and she's a perfectly lovely human being so I guess I'm Satan.

DAVID. You're not competing with her.

SONYA. You want to hear something funny? When I bought her pantyhose she automatically took some from the irregular bin and I didn't even try to talk her out of it. I don't feel guilty about it, either.

DAVID. Neither of us has handled things well with LaShonda but that can change.

SONYA. She's manipulating you.

DAVID. Don't say that. We can make this work. I want you to stay here, too.

SONYA. I have a job, David— my family— I'm not going to live in Indianapolis.

DAVID. It's not forever.

SONYA. I don't even recognize you anymore. I'm going home in the morning, David. I hope you'll come with me but if you don't I'm leaving anyway.

DAVID. Are you leaving me?

SONYA. Don't say that— that's not fair. You're the one who's changing everything.

DAVID. That's true.

SONYA. I'm trying to patient, to understand, but... I'm going back to my life tomorrow— to our life— and if you don't want to come home, fine. But I'm not going to stay in fucking Indianapolis.

DAVID. All right.

SONYA. God— is that it? Aren't you at least going to try to talk me out of it?

(Pause. Then TRUDY knocks and ENTERS.)

THE SAFETY NET

TRUDY. Is something wrong? *(Beat.)* David?
DAVID. No. Nothing's wrong.
TRUDY. Can you come downstairs, then? The Rosens are here.
DAVID. We'll be right there.
TRUDY. Thank you. Are you okay, Sonya?
SONYA. I'm fine.
TRUDY. Good. Everybody's waiting.
DAVID. Mom? Tell Dad not to do that trick where he lights the tissue paper on fire and says it's a Polish rocket. He always forgets Mrs. Rosen is Polish.
TRUDY. *(A beat.)* He hasn't done that for years. See you in a minute.

(She EXITS. Pause.)

SONYA. We need to go downstairs.

(She EXITS without waiting for DAVID.)

(Nine. Lights shift to a tree. LASHONDA standing alone. DAVID ENTERS. Pause.)

LASHONDA. I guess mama gave me up.
DAVID. She said you like to visit Sharron when you're upset. It's hard not talking to you.
LASHONDA. I think he washed away. Last time I was here I could still see some.
DAVID. Ashes, you mean? Well, they're not precisely ashes.
LASHONDA. What?
DAVID. Never mind.
LASHONDA. But it is Sharron down there. I mean, it was

THE SAFETY NET

LASHONDA. It's right.
DAVID. I think that one over there—
LASHONDA. Smell my breath, I'm cold sober. See?
DAVID. Yes.
LASHONDA. I'm never drinking another drop, swear on the Bible.
DAVID. Good.
LASHONDA. Smell me, David, for real; I ain't gonna bite. I want you to believe me.
DAVID. I believe you.
LASHONDA. This is the tree.
DAVID. *(A beat.)* This park is where he used to go when he ran away from home. Up that tree, or one of these trees, with sandwiches and orange juice to wait till I came to get him. Sometimes till after dark if I had band practice. For a while he ran off just about every day.
LASHONDA. For real?
DAVID. It was a game of sorts.
LASHONDA. My boys might run away once. After that their butts be too sore for tree climbing.
DAVID. It was my idea to scatter the ashes here. That was my sole contribution to the festivities.
LASHONDA. Is it true you told him you wrote Star Wars?
DAVID. He mentioned that?
LASHONDA. He said you acted like Star Wars was this story you made up out of your head and Sharron told everybody at school that it was his brother's story— and they were all like first grade or something and they believed him. Till the teacher blew the whistle on you.
DAVID. I got him in trouble?
LASHONDA. But even then he didn't believe her, even after she showed him the movie poster. Sharron said they must've ripped

THE SAFETY NET

you off.

DAVID. I had no idea he remembered that.

LASHONDA. You're all right with Sharron. You always was. Anybody say anything about you, Sharron get in their face like that. Got in my face a couple times. I'm not saying he didn't bitch about you, but any fool could see how he felt.

DAVID. He never said anything like that to me.

LASHONDA. He was gonna call you when we had the baby. He was kinda jacked up about being a daddy before you. Not in a bad way. He was just excited.

DAVID. I don't think I talked to him since my wedding. *(Pause.)* Rick said you went to see that specialist.

LASHONDA. Yeah.

DAVID. And is—

LASHONDA. I'm fine.

DAVID. Good. You can tell him to send me the bill.

LASHONDA. David, I don't need you to save my baby.

DAVID. I know that.

LASHONDA. I gotta give you these.

(Holds out keys.)

DAVID. What's this?

LASHONDA. The keys to my car.

DAVID. It's your car— I bought it for you.

LASHONDA. Just take 'em, okay? I have to go now.

DAVID. How are you going to get home?

LASHONDA. I'll take the bus. I can't see you no more, David.

DAVID. I realize I've been a little harsh, you know, a little controlling, but please forgive me. I didn't mean to hit you.

LASHONDA. I know that. It's nothing; didn't even leave a mark.

DAVID. I just want to talk to you, check in from time to time.

THE SAFETY NET

LASHONDA. I wish it was me you really wanted to talk to. Sharron ain't coming back, you know?
DAVID. I don't see what the car has to do with anything. Sell it if you don't want it. What am I going to do with a car?
LASHONDA. I gotta take care of my own self. Right? No more charity case. Just take 'em, David. *(Beat. DAVID takes the keys.)* I have to go.
DAVID. If you need anything, just tell Rick. I'll get the message.
LASHONDA. You got to leave me alone now.

(She EXITS. DAVID stares at the keys.)

(Ten. Lights shift. DAVID is alone.)

DAVID. I was waiting in line for heaven. *(A beat.)* Actually, that sounds like one of those jokes, doesn't it? "I'm in line for heaven and the priest turns to the rabbi and blah, blah, blah." But this really happened. I mean, in the dream. Anyway, I'm in line for heaven and I'm impatient because I had to pee, really bad, and I was worried because impatience— if it's not a sin, it's at least no virtue, right?— and I was afraid that any sort of impure thoughts could be held against me. So I was trying to ignore my bladder and tick off all my good deeds in my head so they'd be handy if I needed to talk about them— like heaven is a job interview. And then it hit me. I mean, isn't it strange that even in heaven, even with clouds swirling around my feet, I still have to pee? Aren't the concerns of the body supposed to melt away? And not only did I have to pee, but the line was barely moving. So I began to turn on heaven. I began to think, what kind of paradise is it where you have to stand in line to piss? And these angry, frustrated thoughts began to crowd out all the memories of my good deeds. And just when I was about to make a scene, I finally

THE SAFETY NET

got a glimpse of the urinal. That's all there was, one urinal— I don't know what the women were supposed to do— it's funny how many gaps there are in dreams. Anyway, St. Peter was there by the door: a smiling black man handing out towels and aftershave to everybody on their way out. And he had one of those baskets for tips. Large tips, as I remember. Then, finally, the last person in front of me stepped away and I got to the urinal and I went with that great rush, that relief that makes you shudder... I've had orgasms that were less satisfying than a good pee shiver. For thirty or forty seconds there was such peace. Then it was over. So I zipped up, washed my hands, took a towel and some cologne from St. Pete and tipped him a twenty. And I asked him where should I go from here— you know, where's the entrance? And he just smiled and pointed me back to the end of the line, which as I looked at it, seemed to stretch back for miles. So I walked back toward the end, smiling sympathetically at the people still waiting, and noticing that they all looked vaguely familiar though I couldn't place them. *(Beat.)* When I woke up, you know, I realized I'd wet the bed. Which I haven't done for years.

(Eleven. Lights shift to a waiting area. DAVID ENTERS. After a moment DEB ENTERS and stops, surprised to see him.)

DAVID. I wonder if I could have a minute of your time.

DEB. Are you here to serve me papers?

DAVID. I want to apologize for that. I went too far. I understand you're just doing your job.

DEB. You're not the first. I've had people threaten me, call me the worst names in the book. Rolls off my back. But I appreciate the apology.

DAVID. I want you to know that I threw away that list. No detectives— nothing like that.

DEB. Good. I'm sure your client gets impatient waiting for the courts, but...

DAVID. I just have one more question. I was looking at the records yesterday and I noticed the counselor on this adoption was named Deborah. Different last name but I wondered—

DEB. My maiden name.

DAVID. It was careless of me not to notice that before. Such a small town, how many of you can there be?

DEB. Perhaps I should've said something but I didn't want to make things personal.

DAVID. I'm not trying to—

DEB. I've handled hundreds of cases.

DAVID. We've met before, Deb. I'm sure you don't remember; it was years ago, during the adoption. I was the ten-year-old in the corner, reading a book probably, while you went over the particulars with my parents.

(Pause.)

DEB. I should have known.

DAVID. No doubt my mother asked me to look over the documents you gave her, made some fuss over me, the lawyer in the family. My mother has this spiel about the family of achievers—why, her grandfather went to a four-year college and in his day that was quite unusual... This isn't jogging anything.

DEB. I'm sorry.

DAVID. No, it's all right. I didn't remember you either.

DEB. It was a long time ago.

DAVID. And my family isn't as memorable as we think we are. It's one of our many problems.

DEB. There's only so much we can do from our end, of course; the resources are limited.

DAVID. I'm really not implying you made a mistake.

THE SAFETY NET

DEB. I thought—

DAVID. Oh, no. We must've seemed ideal from your point of view. Affluent. Liberal. Filled with enthusiasm— except maybe for the kid in the corner. You made the right decision.

DEB. But obviously something went wrong.

DAVID. My brother died. Driving drunk.

DEB. I'm sorry.

DAVID. Thank you. I didn't really expect you to remember, but I thought I should come clean.

DEB. So all this— the petition;

DAVID. All this was for me, I guess. The truth is I didn't know my brother that well and I was hoping— it sounds crazy— but I was hoping talking to his mother might help me remember.

DEB. I see. But you can understand how she might not want to dredge up the past.

DAVID. Of course. That was my approach, too. Until recently. I didn't want to blame her. I just wanted her to know that her son was loved. Maybe not well enough, but our intentions were good. But she has a right to her privacy.

(Pause.)

DEB. After some time passes you could ask her again. She may change her mind.

DAVID. Maybe I'll do that. Well, I'm sure you have other—

DEB. Did you really file a petition with the court?

DAVID. No. I went over the case law but apparently I don't have any standing without my brother.

DEB. There was a family in here yesterday. Sort of a similar situation to yours. They want to make a petition to the court but they can't afford an attorney.

DAVID. Are you asking me to volunteer?

THE SAFETY NET

DEB. Well, I could call somebody at the Legal Aid Society but they're pretty overwhelmed and, frankly, there's a reason a lot of them are at the Legal Aid Society.

DAVID. I wish I could but I'm going home tomorrow. New York.

DEB. You could do most of it from New York. I mean, you're already familiar with the law.

DAVID. I'm no expert.

DEB. It isn't that time-consuming really— mostly filling out forms— but that sort of thing can be intimidating for people who aren't used to it.

DAVID. *(A beat.)* I guess I could give it a shot.

DEB. Really?

DAVID. As it happens, Deb, filling out forms is my specialty.

DEB. Come with me. I'll get the name for you. *(They EXIT.)*

(Twelve. Lights shift to an airport. Flight announcements on the PA. SONYA is reading a newspaper. DAVID ENTERS and walks by her, rolling a suitcase. She doesn't look up. DAVID sees her, slows, and decides to keep going. He EXITS. A beat. DAVID RE-ENTERS with the suitcase. This time he stops.)

DAVID. Sonya?

SONYA. Oh, my God. David. Hi.

DAVID. Hi. *(They hug awkwardly.)* This is the last place I expected to run into you.

SONYA. I'm sorry?

DAVID. An airport.

SONYA. I've been a lot better about that lately.

DAVID. Good. Good.

SONYA. On your way to Indianapolis?

DAVID. Dallas. Job interview.

THE SAFETY NET

SONYA. You're not with—

DAVID. No. I'm sort of going through an unemployment period. I've been working part time at the legal aid society in Brooklyn.

SONYA. That sounds interesting.

DAVID. Sometimes. Where are you so bravely flying off to today?

SONYA. San Francisco.

DAVID. For the network?

SONYA. I'm...meeting someone.

DAVID. That sort of meeting.

SONYA. It feels weird to talk about it that way. I don't really know him very well.

DAVID. What does he do?

SONYA. Do you really want to know?

DAVID. He's not a lawyer, I hope.

SONYA. No.

DAVID. You've wised up.

SONYA. That remains to be seen. *(Beat.)* Are you still in touch with—

DAVID. LaShonda? Not really. Rick checks in now and then.

SONYA. She's doing okay?

DAVID. Much better. She ended up having a girl, actually.

SONYA. That's wonderful. *(Beat.)* I suppose you've been dying to tell me that.

DAVID. Why?

SONYA. Proves I'm an idiot; proves she was really pregnant. Et cetera.

DAVID. Not at all. The truth is LaShonda doesn't want me within ten miles of that baby.

SONYA. She'll change her mind. I mean, when the child is old enough to understand who you are.

THE SAFETY NET

DAVID. She asked Rick to tell me it's not Gene's kid. Which is, I don't know, probably a lie, but apparently she has a new boyfriend and if all goes well he'll be the father. Less confusion all around, you see?

SONYA. You're kidding.

DAVID. That seems to be the plan. Rick doesn't talk to her as much anymore; the boyfriend doesn't like him. But she passed her exam and she's sober and that's the important thing.

SONYA. I'm sorry.

DAVID. Me too. *(Beat.)* I was back in Indianapolis recently and I ended up going over to Gene's tree and I talked to him. Well, I talked, you know, and imagined he might be listening. I had some vague notion of— of apologizing, I guess, but that's not the right word. I couldn't think of what to say. So I ended up telling him Star Wars again, starting from the top where Luke's adoptive parents are wiped out by Stormtroopers. That was his favorite. I think he loved me, for a time anyway, when he was small and I was still around. Perhaps I helped him through some things in those days: a scary dream here or there, learning his alphabet. It's not much, I guess, but... *(Shrugs.)* When Gene's daughter is old enough, she may have a question or two about her father. You never know, right? Even if I have to send it to her in a letter or something I'm going to make sure she knows about him.

(Pause.)

SONYA. You just have to give LaShonda time.

DAVID. That's what I keep telling myself.

SONYA. *(A beat.)* I actually— I have to run. My plane's already boarded but I always wait until the last minute, you know. I'm not entirely over it.

DAVID. Of course. Have a safe trip.

THE SAFETY NET

SONYA. You, too. And good luck with the interview.
DAVID. Good luck with your...
SONYA. Thanks.
DAVID. He must be special for you to spend five hours on a plane.
SONYA. I guess so. *(Beat.)* They're calling.
DAVID. Right.

(SONYA hugs him lightly and hurries off with her suitcase. DAVID stands there, alone, as the lights fade out.)

THE END

THE SAFETY NET

Prop Plot

ACT I

Scene 1: David's suitcase — Preset on bench SL
Cup of coffee — Preset on the shelf upstage under the mirror
Neck Ties — SR
Toiletries — David — SR

Scene 3: Cardboard box — Preset on Bed SR
Plastic vodka flask — Preset in David's suit jacket
Scrap of paper — Preset in David's pocket
2 plastic cups — Rick enters carrying

Scene 4: Bus fare — Preset on LaShonda's backpack

Scene 5: 3 cups of coffee in a cardboard tray — David enters carrying

Scene 7: 2 textbooks — LaShonda pulls from backpack
1 bag of groceries and 1 bag of clothes — David enters carrying
1 package of pork chops — Preset in grocery bag
Palm Pilot — Preset in David's pants pocket

Scene 8: File folder with forms — Deb brings out with her during scene change

Scene 9: 2 bottles of beer — David enters carrying

Scene 10: Vanilla Candle and matches — Preset on table
2 cans of RC Cola — SL

Scene 11: Pile of folded clothes — Preset on bed

Scene 13: Apartment keys — David SR

THE SAFETY NET

ACT II

Scene 2: Notebook and textbook — Preset on bench
Keys — Preset in backpack
Paper with cell phone number — Preset in David's pants pocket

Scene 3: High School Year Book — Preset on bed
Cardboard box — Preset on floor in front of bed

Scene 4: File folder — Deb brings on with her
Data base sheets — David enters carrying

Scene 5: 2 plastic food trays containing a paper cup, napkin and taco each — LaShonda and Sonya enter carrying

Scene 6: 2 towels and 1 pillow — Preset on bed

Scene 7: Bottle of wine — LaShonda brings on during scene change
3 Plastic wine glasses — Preset on table

Scene 9: Car Keys — Preset on LaShonda's pocketbook

Scene 12: Magazine and suitcase — Sonya brings on during scene change
Rolling Suitcase — David enters rolling

THE SAFETY NET

Costume Plot

DAVID

Act I Scene 1 — charcoal suit, striped shirt, navy tie, dress shoes
Scene 2 — same
Scene 3 — same, tie loosened, no jacket
Scene 4 — same, jacket on
Scene 5 — suit pants, same shirt, sweatshirt
Scene 6 — same
Scene 7 — suit, same shirt, red/navy striped tie
Scene 8 — same
Scene 9 — same, jacket off, no tie
Scene 10 — same, add jacket
Scene 11 — same, jacket off
Scene 12 — same
Scene 13 — suit, light blue tie

Act II Scene 1 — light tan suit, blue checked shirt, tie, dress shoes
Scene 2 — same
Scene 3 — jacket off, no tie
Scene 4 — jacket on, light blue tie
Scene 6 — khakis, bright button up, shoes
Scene 7 — same
Scene 8 — same
Scene 9 — same pants, blue t-shirt
Scene 10 — same
Scene 11 — same, shirt from Scene 2
Scene 12 — same pants, polo shirt

THE SAFETY NET

SONYA

Act I Scene 1 — pink robe, slippers, white tank, blue pj pants
    Scene 5 — suit pants, blue sweater, tan flats
    Scene 13 — same pants, striped shirt, black heels

Act II Scene 5/6 — tan suit, same shoes, black tank, black purse
    Scene 8 — suit pants, top from I. Scene 13, same shoes
    Scene 12 — flowered shirt, white sweater, white shoes

LASHONDA

Act I Scene 4 — jeans, shirt, shoes
    Scene 7 — pj pants, blue tank, sneakers
    Scene 10 — jeans, teal top, black heels

Act II Scene 2 — same jeans, pink striped top, shoes
    Scene 5 — jeans, shirt, shoes
    Scene 7 — jeans, t-shirt, sneakers
    Scene 9 — jeans, sweater, shoes

TRUDY

Act I Scene 3 — tan dress, black slides
    Scene 11 — beige pants, black tank, light blue top, same shoes

Act II Scene 3 — same pants, black top, same shoes
    Scene 6 — same as I. Scene 11
    Scene 8 — black and red jacket, black pants, black camisole, same shoes

RICK

Act I Scene 3 — khaki pants, white shirt, textured-tweed jacket, dress shoes
    Scene 9 — khakis, plaid button up, same shoes

THE SAFETY NET

Act II Scene 3 — same, polo shirt, sneakers
Scene 7 — jeans, t-shirt, same sneakers

DEB

Act I Scene 8 — wool pants, navy blouse, navy shoes, red cardigan

Act II Scene 4/11 — same

THE SAFETY NET

Set Plot

The set consisted of a wall of panels that spun around during scene changes. The panels were textured on one side and dressed on the other side to indicate place with the following items and set moves:

ACT I
Scene 1	Mirror with shelf
Scene 2	Blank wall
Scene 3	Rock Poster (bed)
Scene 4	Street sign
Scene 5	Bed and Breakfast sign (2 chairs)
Scene 6	Blank wall
Scene 7	Photos and newspaper clippings (table, 2 chairs, couch)
Scene 8	Clock
Scene 9	Rock Poster (bed)
Scene 10	Photos and newspaper clippings (table, 2 chairs, couch)
Scene 11	Rock Poster (bed)
Scene 12	Blank wall
Scene 13	Mirror with shelf

ACT II
Scene 1	Blank wall
Scene 2	Street sign
Scene 3	Rock Poster (bed)
Scene 4	Clock
Scene 5	Taco Bell sign
Scene 6	Rock Poster (bed)
Scene 7	Photos and newspaper clippings (table, 2 chairs, couch)

THE SAFETY NET

    Scene 8   Rock Poster (bed)
    Scene 9   Park sign
    Scene 10   Blank wall
    Scene 11   Clock
    Scene 12   Delta Airline sign

*There should be light and sound cues before and after each scene change. The only internal sound cues were a baby crying at the beginning of Act I Scene 7 and Jazz Music that played throughout Act I Scene 10.

THE SAFETY NET

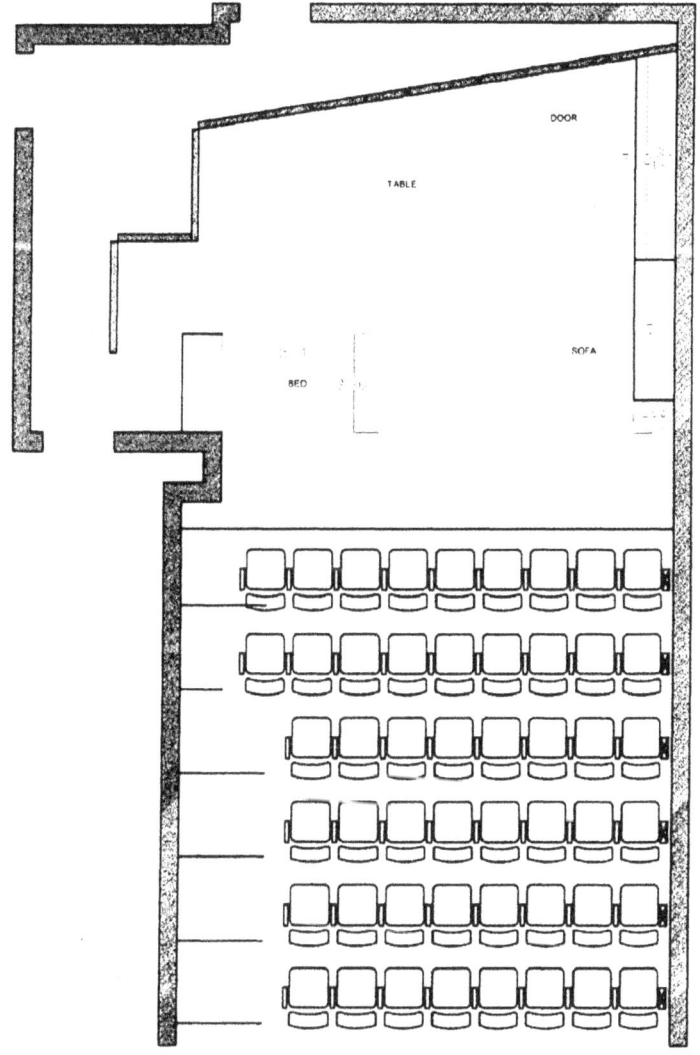

www.ingramcontent.com/pod-product-compliance
Lightning Source LLC
Chambersburg PA
CBHW051409290426
44108CB00015B/2213